The Brontës,
My Mother
and Me

The Brontës, My Mother and Me:

Forgetful wanderings
of love and loss

ANNA M BILEY

BROWN
DOG
BOOKS

Published under licence by Brown Dog Books and
The Self-Publishing Partnership Ltd, 10b Greenway Farm,
Bath Rd, Wick, nr. Bath BS30 5RL, UK

www.selfpublishingpartnership.co.uk

ISBN printed book: 978-1-83952-787-6
ISBN e-book: 978-1-83952-788-3

Cover design by Kevin Rylands
Internal design by Mac Style
Illustrations by Hannah Lee

Printed and bound in the UK

This book is printed on FSC® certified paper

MIX
Paper | Supporting
responsible forestry
FSC® C013604

After nourishment, shelter and companionship, stories are the things we need most in the world (Philip Pullman).

Contents

Acknowledgements   ix

A Labyrinth of Forgetfulness   xiv

Chapter 1   1

Chapter 2   8

Chapter 3   15

Chapter 4   22

Chapter 5   28

Chapter 6   35

Chapter 7   43

Chapter 8   50

Chapter 9   56

Chapter 10   61

Chapter 11   68

Chapter 12   74

Chapter 13   79

Chapter 14   85

Chapter 15   90

Chapter 16   95

Chapter 17   101

Chapter 18   106

Chapter 19   113

Chapter 20   118

Chapter 21   123

Chapter 22   129

Chapter 23   136

Chapter 24   142

Notes   146
Bibliography and References   150

Acknowledgements

To the Brontës and to the scholars, poets and enthusiasts you have inspired. Thank you for your wisdom, vision and guidance.

To bereaved children everywhere. Your stories matter. Thank you.

Special thanks to Hannah Lee for her loving care and creativity and to our very own brown dog gang who have been my constant friends and companions as I wrote this book.

Deepest love and gratitude to my family, to the ancestors and to all who continue to be part of the story. To my sons, thank you for being you. I love you more that words can say.

Song.

"When we were
young, one day.
one beautiful
morning in May"

You told me you told me
you loved me when we
were young one day."

For Rosie

Left holding fragile space
sadness and love exploding
in a magical elixir
Wuthering Heights muddling the mind
Shirley in scrambled forgetfulness
Collides with conjured up
lanterns of Wildfell Hall
and guide my mother's mind.

Be still wild memory
See

Jane Eyre on the breeze
floating aimlessly on the labyrinthine path
Clouds gathering
shapeshifting precious memories
Agnes Grey threads a dizzying
circle of wisdom.
Villette and her Professor
the complexity of heartbreak
and misjudgements of
a bereaved child's frazzled
trust, loss and tragedy
smother dreams and overwhelm.

Ghosts walk.

Brontë women wild and wise
hold my hand and show the way.

A Labyrinth of Forgetfulness

I'm just going to write because I cannot help it.[1]

I come from a line of storytellers, which is remarkable considering the women in my family did not believe they were anything out of the ordinary. Yet their lives were full, revolving around hearth, home and the town's cotton mills, where they would yack on endlessly about the stuff of women and the flaws of men. At first glance in the masculine world in which they were forced to reside, they appeared as voiceless, little people, but it is precisely because of who they were that they made a difference. In *The Life of Charlotte Brontë*, written two years after her death, the author, Elizabeth Gaskell, interviewed local people, those who dwelt on the margins of the lives of the famous family. One such person was the local stationer who noticed that the sisters were frequenting his shop more often:

I have known Miss Brontë a long time; indeed, ever since they came to Haworth in 1819. But I had not much acquaintance with the family till about 1843, when I began to do a little in the stationery line. Nothing of that kind could be had nearer than Keighley before I began. They used to buy a great deal of writing paper, and I used to wonder whatever they did with so much. When I was out of stock, I was always afraid of their coming; they seemed so distressed about it, if I had none. I have walked to Halifax (a distance of 10 miles) many a time for half a ream of paper, for fear of being without it when they came.[2]

And there you have it. A story of the little person, a man whose ordinary life made the extraordinary happen. This is the man who got his boots on and trekked across the Yorkshire moors so that the Brontë sisters had the paper to pen some of the greatest novels ever written. How brilliantly nosey of Mrs Gaskell to find him and to see his part in one of the greatest chapters of English literature. As one of the few female novelists and storytellers of the Victorian era, Elizabeth Gaskell knew to look to the margins and to tune in to the tales of everyday goings-on. Nuggets of treasure can always be found, if only we know where to look. And this is precisely why the little people matter and why the world is a richer place when their stories are told. You may wonder, dear reader, how I dare attempt to write a book that incorporates the blessed Brontës. Forgive me. I know that I tread on hallowed ground, made sacred by Sylvia Plath, Ted Hughes, Virginia Woolf and all Brontë writers, poets and academics who have fed my passion and been my inspiration for as long as I can remember. However, I stand on the shoulders of the little people: the stationer of Haworth and the librarian of a small provincial Lancashire town, who introduced my mother to *Wuthering Heights*.

I am a Brontë enthusiast, born and bred, with a story that comes from the heart, of how the three sisters, Emily, Anne and Charlotte mattered – to me and to my mother. The myth of the Brontës is woven into my life. Growing up in a Brontë world, we walked the hills where Heathcliff and Cathy roamed and played hide and seek among the green hollows and moss-covered ruins of Jane Eyre's Ferndean Manor. Stoked by my mother, reality merged into myth and myth into reality. All of it was true to us, and if it wasn't, what did it matter? What is more, the lives of the Brontë sisters and the essence of characters such as Jane Eyre, Helen Graham and Nellie Dean, reflected what I saw among my own women folk. With grit and truth, these northern women were strong both in character and common sense. Fiercely protecting their own and yet with arms and bosoms full of nurturing kindness, their voice, resilience, creativity, loyalty and love defined womanhood. This is not a story of historical fact and rigor but a tale of how Emily, Charlotte and Anne shaped lives, thinking and ambition. These women burned with passion and a feisty northernness. They brimmed with genius and a breathtaking vision that inspired. Quite simply, in our house, they were family.

In the last few years of her life, like so many women of the war generation, my mother became increasingly forgetful. A kindly doctor informed her that she had what was called age onset memory loss, that she was simply forgetful, and it was only to be expected in someone of her age. Unlike many of her lifelong school friends and neighbours, who were packaged and dispatched to care homes, my mother was never diagnosed with dementia. And yet, her mind was muddled, as if the filing cabinet of memory had been ransacked, the contents thrown up in the air, abandoned to float aimlessly on the breeze and land randomly out of space and time. As little mistakes, memory lapses and slip-ups became more frequent, she would flippantly bat away these hiccups and chirp, 'It's my age you know', or 'That's old age and poverty for you'.

Happy or sad, joyful or angry, in my mother's book, hormones and age were the devious culprits, blamed for all ills, misjudgements, emotional mood swings and forgetfulness. Exploding teenagers, tearful, premenstrual young women and middle-aged, overwhelmed daughters, were all excused and explained away by their age. In their later years, gentlemen may be described as eccentric or absent-minded, whereas women become scatty, batty old dears, the butt of family jokes and the epicentre of family frustration. Stories, simple instructions and daily routines whirl around in circles, wearing away the frazzled threads of adult children's patience, so often sandwiched between their own troubled darlings and ageing parents.

Forgetfulness is a sneaky creature. It ebbs and flows, shapeshifting into everyday routines, disrupting plans, creeping into sleep patterns, smothering dreams and then disappears in a puff of smoke. Elusive and complex, forgetfulness cannot be diagnosed or pinned down as an illness to be treated. It is just there, playing mischief with memory and muddling the mind. Like a phantom, it comes and goes, challenging reality and what we think we know. Over time, forgetfulness falls over itself, as its tangling tricks burrow deeper into the core of self, teasing out the agonising question: who am I now? Looking on from a place of their own confusion and heartbreak, adult children may ask where the parent they knew has gone and at what point did they start to take their leave. With no diagnosis except for 'old age', there is little support for the forgetful and even less guidance for loved ones, left holding the fragile space of sadness, frustration, despair and love.

Journeying with my mother, as memory loss edged her towards the end of life, was as if I was walking a labyrinth. The ancient, circular path, trodden by civilisations in every part of the globe, represents the conundrum of human existence, the quest to find meaning and purpose in life and death. The labyrinth is a puzzle, aimed both to scramble the mind and to show the way. Unlike a maze, there is one path in and out of a labyrinth. Trust the path and you will find your way. I was on a path, a trajectory of forgetfulness and frailty, that was going in one direction, towards my mother's death. I had walked this way many times before as a nurse and also with my husband, who died of cancer. The path was familiar as I anticipated the uncertain twists and turns of events that come with the end of life, bereavement and grief. And yet it was new and sad in a way I had never experienced, for, at the end of the path, my life would change forever, as I morphed into an adult bereaved child, a motherless daughter. My mother too was on her own labyrinthine path, negotiating life and death, in a way blurred by memory loss. Imagining my mother's mind as a labyrinth of forgetfulness, I pondered how this was for her. What patterns did she see? How did it feel? Where was meaning and purpose, and how did she find her way?

One of the most familiar stories in Greek mythology is the tale of the minotaur. This ugly, vicious beast, half-man, half-bull, dwelt in a labyrinth beneath the palace of King Minos of Crete and feasted on human sacrifice. The brave, young hero of the story, Theseus, volunteered to put an end to the evil. The king's daughter, Ariadne, happened to be in love with our hero, and she gave him a ball of red thread to help him find his way out of the labyrinth. Theseus slayed the minotaur and with the thread to guide him, made a quick exit from the labyrinth and ran off back to Athens with Ariadne. On the way, he abandoned her on a Greek island, and it all ended in tears and tragedy.[3] Reflecting on this Greek myth of labyrinth, I am drawn to the gift of the red thread as a metaphor to illustrate that we all need help and something or someone to guide us along the way.

For my mother, the thread in the labyrinth of her forgetfulness was a diary, in which she concurrently relived memories of the past and attempted to hold on to every day. Flowing in and out to the centre of her memories, the diary connected my mother to self and helped her remember who she was and the girl she had been. It was a path she knew well for it was the pattern of her life. She could not get lost because she was home. At the turn of the labyrinth, where memory and forgetfulness collided were my mother's parents, beloved aunts, uncles, loved ones long dead. Conjured up in a magical elixir, they became real once again, and I, the living, was the ghost – the unreal, intangible one.

For four generations, my family have been rooted in Brontë country. The lives of Charlotte, Emily, Anne and brother Branwell were a source of fascination and inspiration for my mother. So often she would say that they had been there before us and 'knew what it was to have a hard life'. Not surprising then that they too were among the precious memories that she revisited time and again as she recalled her younger life. On the path of forgetfulness, the Brontë sisters brought to life the characters from their novels. *Jane Eyre, Wuthering Heights, Agnes Grey, The Tenant of Wildfell Hall, Shirley, Villette* and *The Professor* were not only cherished stories but also my mother's guide to life, rooting and reminding her that she belonged in the wild, tempestuous landscape of Brontë country on the Lancashire/Yorkshire border.

This book is an invitation to walk a labyrinth of forgetfulness, love and loss with the Brontës, my mother and me. Navigating the twists and turns of the labyrinth's mossy path, there will be slips and trips along the way. Hold my hand, dear reader, as we 'see the black clouds gathering round my native hills'.[4] In dizzying circles, from girl to parent to child once more, the labyrinth of memory took my mother to the edge of life and death, and back again, until, in the early hours of a November morning, she stepped across the threshold. Do not be afraid. Across time and place, we may fall into hidden potholes of grief and sadness, but have no fear, for the wise ones are waiting with lanterns of wisdom and wry humour to guide us. Let us be still and watch the weather come in over the wild expanses of Brontë country. And perhaps, in the labyrinth of forgetfulness and memory, we may find a new story of patience, kindness and mother–daughter love.

Chapter 1

These eyes in the Evening Star you must have seen in a dream. How could you make them look so clear, and yet not at all brilliant? For the planet above quells their rays. And what meaning is that in their solemn depth? And who taught you to paint wind?[5]

'Read Wuthering Heights when you're eighteen and you think Heathcliff is a romantic hero; when you're thirty, he's a monster; at fifty you see he's just human'.[6] I first read *Wuthering Heights* at the age of fourteen. It was 1977 and the ghost of Cathy was Kate Bush, floating about in a white gothic style nightdress on *Top of the Pops*. I remember being shocked that my mother would have recommended such a violent, passionate, angst-ridden book. But, for her, it was about soul, humanity, landscape and home. My mother knew a good thing when she saw it and, in her wisdom, discerned that the Brontë novels were destined to be a rite of passage to womanhood for me, in the same way they had been for her. At the age of fifty, *Wuthering Heights*, and indeed all the Brontë writings, became a personal guide and friend through grief and bereavement as I found myself a widow and single mother. The women, fictitious and real, who survived against the odds and who found love on their terms, continued to walk with me as I cared for, loved and let go of my mother. But my love of storytelling didn't begin with her, and so, as Mrs Gaskell famously wrote, let us 'begin with the old rigmarole of childhood'.[7]

As one of five siblings, all now middle-aged, we often speak of childhood memories, of the parents, grandparents, neighbours and friends who shared our lives in the Lancashire mill town where we grew up. Side by side, all at once and all equally valid, there are five different versions of childhood. Each of us have our own unique memories of that time, of the same mother and father, of what mattered and what didn't, the things that make up happy memories and the things that still hurt. We all have our own stories to tell. Mine is that of growing up in a Cranford world of old ladies and busybodies.[8]

One of my earliest memories is of a thumbnailed fan of clipped brown feathers on the velvet band of a green, felt cloche hat. It complemented a wool coat of the same colour, with a diamante owl brooch perched on its high, gaping collar. The large amber eyes of the curious creature staring down at the tiny child sent her scurrying behind the sofa. Tottering across the room with a *clip, clip* of misshaped, shiny, laced, brown leather shoes, a tall lady stooped and reached out to the child. Her ancient face, caked in pale powdered make-up, broke into a smile that lit up her dark eyes. 'And what is your name?' asked the lady, reaching out a twisted hand. It was warm and she smelt of sweet-scented perfume. 'Nell,' I squeaked. 'Pleased to meet you Nell. I am Mrs Rushworth,' she said. 'I live in the house next door. You and your mam must come and see me tomorrow. I'll have some chocolate biscuits ready for you.'

And so, as the tale unfolded over tea, I learnt that this woman had moved into our old lady street, to be near her sister, who we knew as Auntie Annie. She was no relation to us whatsoever but was a friend of my Granny Vi who lived a few doors further down the road. Auntie Annie was a kind, quiet, simple soul. Her dress, hair and heavily rimmed spectacles were grey and unassuming – her home, similarly self-effacing. Gently tapping the brass fox head door-knocker with one hand and clinging to my mother's neck in an attempt to steady my fretfulness with the other, we were to discover that Mrs Rushworth and her home were very different indeed. As the door opened, the sweet-old-lady smell once again wafted towards me. The cheeky owl had been replaced by a sparkling spray of tiny, enamelled stars, pinned to the bosom of a flowing cream-coloured blouse. The faint pink lines in her wool, pleated brown skirt blended with cerise pink slippers. My three-year-old eye was once again drawn to the curved shape of her footwear, igniting further curiosity about this strange woman. It wasn't until later that I came to learn it was not her shoes but her feet that were misshapen. This was caused by a grown-up thing called bunions, which were cripplingly painful and no laughing matter.

The only living room in the cottage was tiny and packed with brightly coloured ornaments of dancing ladies; painted, smiling dogs and lines of blue patterned jugs and plates on shelves of polished mahogany. Treasures of fancy cups and saucers and a collection of porcelain thimbles were stored in an oak corner cabinet behind a locked glass door. Over the fireplace, there was a framed painting of purple, green and blue hills, later to be known as the Lake District picture. To the left, there was an enormous, black-framed, pencil drawing of a young Victorian lady and gentleman, obviously in love. To the right, the same couple, now an aged top-hatted gentleman and a sweet-faced matron in a laced cap and gown. But the most intriguing of all the artwork was a pencilled sketch of a scruffy old dog, curled in sleep. Pointing to it, Mrs Rushworth proudly told us that it was a drawing of King Edward VII's dog, Caesar, and the writing on it read *Man's Best Friend*. This newly discovered emporium was fascinating and delightful but, as ever, in my young world, there was anxiety. The stress and pressure to be a good girl, to never say or do anything that might make a grown-up cross, was omnipresent. From the kitchen, Mrs Rushworth brought in and placed before me a glass of milk and a plate with three chocolate biscuits. In our house, shop-bought biscuits (especially chocolate ones) were birthday and special occasion treats. As the youngest of then four children, the realisation that they were all for me and didn't have to be shared, was pure joy.

Over time, Mrs Rushworth became my beloved Rusha. On rainy afternoons, she would take me to her house where I would stand on a small wooden buffet and watch her baking. If I resisted the temptation to dip my fingers in the creamy, golden mixture, I was allowed to lick the spoon before helping with the washing up. Sometimes, I was invited to lend a hand folding the laundry, or she might give me a cloth and I would be her busy assistant, polishing a precious collection of brass and silver ornaments. However, it was rooting through Rusha's jewellery box that brought the most honour and excitement. Proudly showing me her collection of glitzy brooches, necklaces and earrings, many of which had belonged to her mother and grandmother, Rusha told stories of long ago. Her grandfather had been a sea captain in the days when ships, donned with billowing white masts, rope and rigging, were powered by the wind. As a little girl of seven, her mother accompanied her parents on a voyage to Australia. Playing with a huge tin of old-fashioned buttons taught me about counting and colours and in discovering the odd shiny brass button, I came to know that there had been a Mr Rushworth who had been in the army and was dead. Undead, but living in a far-off land called India, was another Mr Rushworth, her son Frederick, who had a very important job of working for the government. Through Rusha, her stories and lovingly preserved old photographs, my world began to open and stretch out beyond the old lady street, to imagine far-flung places and people beyond the end of the road.

The wonderful thing about Rusha was that she was mine, and I didn't have to share her with my brothers and sister. I cannot remember the backdrop to why I spent so much time with her, but it is unimportant. With her, I was safe and happy, chattering, playing, trotting alongside, holding her hand and trusting her totally. On one occasion, I accompanied Rusha to the local park to see the Salvation Army Brass Band. Other times, we would take the bus to the market or go to tea parties and coffee mornings where there were other hatted, trinket accessorised, sweet-smelling ladies with lashings of powdered make-up masking their wrinkled, white faces. It was there, as the outlier, the observer child, that I fell in love with old ladies and their stories. But it was all a mystery. I sat quietly, watching and listening to these women, with no concept that one day I would be one. I had cake, biscuits and Rusha all to myself. That was enough.

To have well-behaved children was something that my parents valued highly. Rusha reported to everyone that our Nell was a polite little girl, with excellent manners and was a pleasure to take anywhere. That made them happy and me, well, less anxious for a moment or two. With awe and wonder, I looked up to the adults in my world, who somehow always knew when to say please and thank you, to hold doors open for others, when to speak, when to keep schtum and when to give way one's seat on a bus. To my tiny self, they seemed so knowledgeable, proud, dignified and comfortable in their world. Silently, from behind the sofa, I watched, listened and learnt about life and about women. There was Miss Gladys Grubb (poor thing), who walked a cat on a lead. There was Mrs Yates with her drawn-on eyebrows and the whist-playing 'Mona by name and Mona by nature', another poor, abandoned, round-spectacled Miss.

Sociable, caring and intelligent, these strangely beautiful creatures were also collectively cruel. As close as sisters, these women were fiercely protective of home, of all they had fought and worked for and, ultimately, of each other. And yet, beneath the multicoloured feathers of their fancy hats, these old ladies, like a murder of crows, could also argue and screech like scavengers as they picked over the carcasses of rule breakers and the fallen.

By the time I was six, many people had come and gone in my short life. I have snippets of vivid memories of my grandfathers. They were there, then they weren't. No one ever said where they had gone or why. For a short time, my parents were emergency foster carers. Babies and children came and went. One day they were there and then they disappeared with no explanation or chance to say goodbye. One sunny Saturday, Mrs Rushworth and Auntie Annie set off for a holiday in Cornwall. It was all very exotic and exciting. My dad drove them to the railway station, and I was allowed to go with him. Enthusiastically planting kisses on my hand and waving them away, as the train slowly pulled out, my Rusha disappeared out of sight. I never saw her again. My parents got a phone call from Auntie Annie to say that Edith (apparently that was her name) had died. I have never forgotten the day of my first bereavement. It was the first time my heart broke.

On reflection, it is interesting to see how the old ladies of my Cranford world shaped my life. They taught me to hear the unspoken, to read between the lines, to observe the finest of detail and to feel the power of love and loyalty. They taught me to paint the wind. Eventually becoming a nurse, unsurprisingly, my love of old ladies propelled me into a career caring for the elders of society. A privilege and honour, these years of service were hard work and so much fun. As if it was yesterday, I remember our street on the edge of industrial Lancashire, where my parents lived for over fifty years.

Transitioning, from being the parents of a young family to the old folk of the neighbourhood, grandparents and great-grandparents, they were woven into the fabric of lives and landscape in that little corner of England. The ancients, the wise old crones, had been there forever and a day … until one day they weren't.

Chapter 2

A calm day had settled into a crystalline evening; the world wore a North Pole colouring: all its lights and tints looked like the reflets* of white, or violet, or pale green gems. The hills wore a lilac-blue; the setting sun had a purple in its red; the sky was ice, all silvered azure; when the stars rose, they were of white crystal – not gold; gray or cerulean, or faint emerald hues – cool, pure, and transparent – tinged the mass of the landscape.[9]

The only sliver of light on a darkened road was the silver reflection of headlights on blackened puddles. Shouldered and protected from the night and the rain by towering dry stoned walls, a car twisted along the narrow lanes, swerving to avoid a stray stone as it stumbled from its lofty height, down steep rooted banking, and thudded into a stagnant ditch. The car spluttered as it dropped a gear to climb the last steep stretch and, as lights came into view, indicated, and swung into a small, congested car park. This road was as familiar as the noduled, twisted veins on the back of my proverbial hand and, like blood to the heart, was taking me home. Stepping out of the car, the only sign of light was from the inside of an ancient inn; immediately, the sickly smell of warmed chips and vinegar reminded me that I was hungry after a long, seven-hour drive up country. Struggling to drag my small, wheeled suitcase across the gravel of the muddied, pot-holed car park, I pushed my way through a studded oak door and was hit by the welcoming warmth of a huge log fire, burning in the arch of an ancient fireplace. 'Hiya, love. Back again?' the old barman enquired. 'Yeh,' I replied with a weak smile, 'back again.' Back again.

The familiar pub was empty except for a couple, huddled and canoodling in a dark corner and three men, standing at the bar, nursing their pints of bitter. 'You are in room four tonight, love,' the barman said, handing me a key, attached to a red leather cricket ball keyring. It was the oddest thing and although I had stayed at this inn many times, I had never asked why, nor had I been let in on the joke. Thanking him, I turned and struggled my suitcase up a narrow, panelled staircase and along the short corridor to my room. But alas, amidst the skirmish with bags and the paraphernalia of coat, handbag and car keys, I could not find the cricket ball. How was that possible? It was massive. Almost in tears of frustration and exhaustion I retraced my steps to find it on the bar where I had left it. One of the men, now perching on a tall stool, turned and (smirking to his mates) said, 'Thou'st forget thi 'ed if it were loose, love.' Laughing along, I agreed, whilst inwardly grumbling, 'smart arse…'

The corridor was draughty. Opening the door, I fumbled along the wall for the light switch and was hit by the quiet chill of the room. An icy shudder gripped my heart as the creepy sight came into view. A deep windowsill, one corner stacked with mottled books and dog-eared maps, framed small, stone mullioned windows and beyond, in the pitch-black night I heard the scratch of branches against the window and a distant screech of an owl. 'Oh my God, it's Wuthering Heights.' I rapidly drew the heavy cream curtains before the child ghost of Cathy smashed through the glass and reached out her tiny, frozen hand to grab me. With the night shut out the space was cosy, even luxurious and I indulged in a hot shower and the lavishness of a posh warmed dressing gown. Too tired and too tight to pay for room service, I opened a can of cheap white wine fizz and dined on leftover service station cheese and pickle sandwiches and a bag of crisps. Flicking around the television channels to find some hypnotic trash, out of the corner of my eye I saw the waft of curtains and shivered, imagining what or who might lie behind it:

> I heard distinctly the gusty wind, and the driving of the snow; I heard, also, the fir-bough repeat its teasing sound … my fingers closed on the fingers of a little, ice-cold hand! The intense horror of nightmare came over me; I tried to draw back my arm, but my hand clung to it, and a most melancholy voice sobbed, *'let me in – let me in … I'm come home, I'd lost my way on the moor'.*[10]

It was still dark when a soft hand woke me, reaching out from a white light, gently touching, and stroking my hair. I recognised the tiny form, the creases and livered spots, the thinning gold wedding band and diamond ring, blackened with age and life and love. It was the hand of my mother, and today was her funeral.

Lying there, alone in a huge, unfamiliar bed, my head nested in feather soft pillows. Toasty warm and snuggled in crispy white, faux-flower-scented sheets, my body uncurled and stretched, unstiffening weary limbs that somehow signalled that, in spite of sleep, I was exhausted. A frosty nose reminded me of the igloo-like quality of the hotel room and reawakened memories of childhood and life before the luxury of central heating. Instinctively, I drew the sheets over my head, to steal a few more moments of warmth and comfort. Rooted in early years and my mother's obsessions, my hatred of the cold made me into a woman who took to thermal underwear long before her time and who, on summer days wears layers of clothes and takes 'just in case' cardigans, sweaters and coats, even on the shortest trips.

My earliest memory of feeling cold was when I was three years old. I was sitting, shivering in a hole in a wall, where a stone fireplace was being built. We lived in an antiquated hand loom weaver's cottage that was built in the 1700s, a house that 21st-century estate agent would probably describe as, 'in need of modernisation'. My dad bought it for ninety pounds, an extortionate amount of money in 1962. The story goes that his father, my grandad, thought he had lost his senses and didn't speak to him for a year. However, being a man who always saw the potential in every situation, Dad was never to regret the decision, although it left him broke for many years. Driven to provide a home for his ever-increasing family he set to work, restoring an almost derelict house, and building his dream. The hand looms were long gone but rusted, iron hooks in oak beams, still hung in the attic, where the weavers and their families, had worked their trade. At least that is what we were told, and as the attic became my bedroom, I much preferred this version of history to the sinister and spooky alternative yarn, peddled by my brothers. Like my father, I loved that house and always have. When I think of home, my heart takes me there.

Whatever the season, our house, on the edge of nowhere was always of a subzero temperature. With stone walls, two feet thick and small, east facing windows, it was freezing. I kid you not when I say that as a child I slept beneath a heap of old, dog smelling coats on the bed. In winter, clothes were folded neatly in a pile under the pillow so I could dress before venturing out of my warm nest, especially on days when a swirling pattern of frost formed both on the inside and outside of the fragile, single-paned glass windows. Reflecting on the softie I had become, I smiled with dawning realisation. Without insight or awareness, I had become my mother, whose preoccupation with battling the elements made me the laughing stock of the school, with her hand knitted and crocheted hats, gloves, jumpers and vests. There was even one occasion when, much to the bewilderment of the other children, the six-year-old Nell was made to wear a woollen liberty bodice. Where on earth my mother sourced this ancient undergarment, I will never know, but fortunately I grew out of it quickly, and that particular embarrassment was short lived. Imagining how this amusing tale would be something to evoke memories for my now eighty-eight-year-old mother, a skip of my heavy heart reminded me that this was the day we gathered to bury her. Back to reality with a resounding thud, the memory softened and thawed. Reluctantly I reached out for the sumptuous, scrumptiously soft bath robe and climbed out of bed. This was the inevitable day I had been dreading all my life. The day I said goodbye.

Padding barefoot across the room, I pulled back the heavy curtains. And there it was. The panoramic landscape, the view I loved and cherished more than any other, that had welcomed me into the world and was my mother's last. This wilderness pulled me, uprooted me, tied me to this place; the moody, possessive scene that I could not shake off, the place that wouldn't let me go. Like a joint sliding back into place under the healing hands of an osteopath, my soul slipped back into a space that was home. I breathed it in and smelt its earthiness. Boulsworth Hill. The highest point of the South Pennine Hills, Boulsworth is a seamless border of patchworked green and brown fields, wild bracken and cloud. Threading across the landscape there are terraces of stone cottages, blackened with age and encrusted filth from the smoke of long-gone cotton mills. Rain-soaked slate roofs, knitted together like the Great Wall of China, weave across the harsh terrain. And yet, what is continuous to the naked eye, in the hearts and minds of local folk lie matters of principle and identity. As the county boundary, Boulsworth demands allegiance to the Red Rose of Lancashire or the White Rose of Yorkshire. You are one or t'other. You cannot be both.

As dawn broke on that dark November morning, the giant that was Boulsworth began to stir. The sleepy, dusky backcloth to my life awakened, and like shifting theatre scenery, seemed to move further away and out of reach as the light played her daily tricks with the rising sun. Of these moors, in the poem *High Waving Heather*, Emily Brontë wrote:

> Darkness and glory rejoicingly blending
> Earth rising to heaven and heaven descending.[11]

For this is Brontë country, the home of Emily, Anne, Charlotte and Branwell. Motherless and within their own fantasy world, *Boulshill* was their playground and the backdrop to the childhood juvenilia of the Glasstown and Angrian sagas.[12] It is the landscape in which the Brontë literary work and myth is rooted, the home and inspiration of *Wuthering Heights* and the marker that forever tells me that I too am home. I thought of my mother and how, every morning, every day, she would look out on the 'grand' views towards Boulsworth and beyond. As if that were not enough, at the day's end and the drawing of curtains, a disproportionate, enormous picture of Top Withins hung over the mantelpiece in a heavy gilded frame.

After a tepid breakfast of cornflakes and toast, I checked out of the inn. Squally, perishing gusts rattled through the bare branches of twisted trees, becoming one with the voice of my mother, telling me to wrap up warm, for it is one of those 'North-Pole days … the sky looks like ice; the earth is frozen; the wind is as keen as a two-edged blade'.[13] In a few hours' time, at her funeral, I would speak of my mother's love of home, the Heights and the moor. As her child-size coffin was lowered in the wintry earth of Lancashire, she would be laid to rest with my father. Her beloved, childhood sweetheart, their souls once again free to roam and find eternal peace among the foothills of Boulsworth. Haworth and the Heights are 'nowt but a cock-stride' and if you 'get your skates' on you can walk it there and back in a day.

an uprooted soul, threading twisted trees,
slipped back home to Wuthering Heights

Chapter 3

Sometimes our mother would amuse us with stories and anecdotes of her younger days, which, while they entertained us amazingly, frequently awoke – in me at least – a vague and secret wish to see a little more of the world.[14]

Her window looked out onto an ancient, twisted sycamore tree and yonder, to a never-ending landscape of moorland, to Brontë country – a view she had loved and cherished all her life. Frail and ailing, her world had shrunk. The space in which she had come to dwell was marked by an electrically operated bed, a matching pine set of drawers and wardrobe cupboards and an open door, leading to a small bathroom. Her bird-like, tiny, cancer-ridden body had determined the physical boundaries of her world, but my mother's mind and memory knew no limitations. On her 86th birthday, she was given a notebook and pen, a gift that sparked her waning imaginings. Through storytelling and diary keeping, her mind was free to roam across time and place. It was as if she found a new voice to process eight decades of living, to work through the losses of family, community, a way of life and female opportunity. As past merged into present and back again, I bore witness to unfolding moments of loving care and compassion as the end of life grew closer. Moreover, my mother's relentless note-keeping became a gentle invitation to glimpse the lived experience and reality of the onset of forgetfulness and memory loss. Or perhaps what I saw was the tender gift that comes with frailty, that of memories gained and remembered, to make the unbearable and the inevitable possible. Virginia Woolf's observation, 'I who am perpetually making notes in the margin of my mind',[15] reflected my mother's story, as she wrote both to hold on to precious memories of the past and to ground herself in the mundane happenings of the everyday.

Born into slums and poverty in 1930s northern England, as a young girl, my mother lived through the Second World War. As a teenager, she saw the introduction of the Welfare State and National Health Service, her beloved NHS. Twenty years later, she gathered her own children around her to witness the giant leap for mankind, as Neil Armstrong stepped out onto the moon in July 1969. Living through economic depression and war, my mother was of a generation that would come to know prosperity beyond childhood imagination, as cars, washing machines, colour televisions and holidays abroad became the norm. But her life was, she thought, unremarkable, never considering herself special or someone with anything to say. How wrong she was. The lives of that remarkable generation mattered. They were the eyewitnesses to the lived social history of the 20th century, and their voices deserve to be heard.

Along with other working-class weaver girls of the industrial north, my mother's destiny was to marry. The hardship she knew in her early years became grist for the mill of life and part of the wisdom that made her who she was. Our elders carry with them a unique imprint of history, knowledge and insight, through which future generations may come to understand who they are. It is our honour to celebrate lives well lived and a privilege to weep with them in loss and grief, as they deal with regrets and unfinished business at the ending of their days. If only we could take time out of our busy 21st-century lives to be alongside them, to listen and share their memories and secrets. Perhaps we may offer a notebook and pen, so these precious wise ones may journal when they are lonely, and alone with their thoughts and memories in the closing of the sacred circle of life and death.

Born in the spring of 1931 in a small industrial textile town in Lancashire, little Rosalie O'Riley was a child of the Second World War. In her almost nine decades, she was known to most people as Our Rosie or Auntie Rose, but to me, she was Mum. Of Irish Catholic and Welsh descent, her parents Violet and Dan came to the town as young children when, as economic migrants, their parents moved to find work in one of the many cotton mills. For over a century, my roots have spanned across this town. Walk with me through the lanes and ginnels of my mother's childhood, along the steep cobbled streets lined with murky stone terrace houses and archaic weavers' cottages. Let me show you the old toll house where Granny Vi lived with her parents, Alice and Charlie Kelly. Down the street and across the park is a towering stone wall, the boundary to the cricket club. Vi's earliest memory was of her da carrying her in his arms alongside the very same wall that is there today. It was 1907, and she was two years old.

Past the park and on to the centre of town, my mother's birthplace is now a car park. Opposite, the building of the public baths and swimming pool stands neglected, its purpose forgotten, except in memory. Of this place, our Rosie wrote in her diary:

> my dad used to tease me that I was born in a circus. It was a flat above a shop in Ludgate Circus. I remember my mother holding me on the windowsill and me, dancing for my dada coming home. Before I started school I was playing on the doorstep when my mother snatched me inside. A herd of cattle had lost their way between the market and slaughterhouse. They couldn't find their way in or out. My mother was in a right palaver.

In Ludgate Circus, in a flat above a grocer's shop that was her first home, the bath was a dolly tub in front of the fire. When they had the ha'penny to spare, little Rosie remembered her parents, trotting across the road, rolled towel under arm, to enjoy the luxury of a weekly bath.

Down Windy Bank and taking a short cut through the snicket at Cabbage Lane, I can show you the steep cobbled streets and point to a building that used to be the Catholic church. My grandparents were the last to marry there before it became a school. I remember it as a vile place, with spider-ridden, outside toilets. Terrifying nuns patrolled the queues of desperate, wriggling kids, distributing to each child, one sheet of medicated toilet paper. My mother's response to this frequent childhood complaint was that we didn't know we were born. 'At least you have flushing toilets,' she would say. For in her day, toilet paper was a square of old newspaper and the rat-infested, tippler toilets, shared with the rest of the street, stank.

Moving quickly on. There to the right is Buckcroft, where my mother used to go with her clay pipe-smoking, clog-dancing Grandma Kitty to visit some poor soul, an elderly, widowed lady who had taken to her bed. She had no carpets or other furniture, and her only decoration was newspaper cuttings from the First World War, spread across the walls. Her one child, a son, had been killed in the war and, at the end of her life, her only support was that of other widow women and grieving mothers. In Rosie's childhood memory, the grim reality of the First World War was raw, still casting its ugly shadow across the town, rumbling like a dark, thunder cloud and colliding with the fear of looming unrest in Europe. Following the main road, through the town and down the hill, the grand columns of the Grecian style War Memorial, made of white Portland stone stand out against the dark Victorian architecture of this industrial Lancashire town. I am sure that was the aim, to honour the dead, kith and kin, with the best that folk could afford. For many years, I had looked but never seen this cenotaph. On each of the columns, name after name of the fallen. I realise how many of them are familiar: Shuttleworth and Shackleton, Laycock and Lund, Hartley and Heaton, Petty and Pickles. These are the ancestors of friends and neighbours, names my mother recalled time and again as she remembered her younger self. The many generations of families, born in this town, died … God only knows where. The memorial reminds me that one of them was a great-grandfather. He lies forever unknown in a Flanders field, and I ponder if he is at peace or does his soul long to be at rest, folded into the familiar landscape of home?

Behind the cenotaph is the old library. Now fancy residential apartments, the library was built in 1907 by the Carnegie Trust as a public facility to make books available to all. Throughout her life, my mother loved that building. She would often reminisce how as a girl she visited the library on her way home from school and 'read a book a day'. Who knows if this was an exaggeration, but her love of books and reading and her dreams of becoming a teacher were rooted in that place. The detour to the library came at a price, and the memory of punishment for being late home, book in hand, was something our Rosie never forgot.

Across the road and taking a sharp left turn round the corner, we come to Auntie Mary's in Dune Street. She was the childminder of the family, taking in her siblings' kids for a few pennies a day so that they could work in the mills. On Sundays, little Rose loved to walk up Winewall, an out of the way hamlet as winding as it sounds, where tiny, gritstone cottages still cling to the edges of the steep, narrow lanes. There she would visit Auntie Elsie and Uncle Horace. They had an allotment, and my mother's job was to return home with fresh vegetables, so scarce in those days. Pushing on a little further and edging along the beck towards Waterside, I can show you the site of the cotton mill where most of my grandparents and great-grandparents worked all their lives. And finally on to the mill where my mother first went to work at the age of fourteen, the year the war ended. Next to it was an Italian Prisoner of War camp. The men used to whistle at the weaver girls as they would come and go in and out of the mill. 'They were a cheerful lot,' my mother would say. But that was long ago. It is a supermarket now.

Through a collective love of family and storytelling, I learned about my bloodline – none of it shiny, but all of it evoking a strange curiosity about the bullying men and feisty women I am descended from. For example, Charlie Kelly, a maternal great grandfather, was a drunk and a bad 'un. On a regular basis, he beat his wife and children with a brass buckled belt. As a young woman in the 1920s, Vi took the daring step of having her hair cut in a fashionable bob style, and he beat her black and blue. He struck his wife for the last time when our Vi intervened, knocking him out cold with an iron poker. He never touched either of them again and disappeared for many years, only to return sick and dying. Violet took him in, made room for him in the front parlour and nursed him until the end, such was her big heart, her loyalty and ability to forgive. With a northern frankness, the Brontë sisters wrote of strong resilient women whose lot in life was to go from deathbed to deathbed, caring for sick and stricken relatives and neighbours. So it was in my ancestral line. Granny Vi was what today we would call that 'go to' person, alongside women in childbirth, caring for the new-born, the dying and who laid out the dead. 'Because that's what families do,' my mother often said. They protect, they shelter and they love.

With an age gap of eighteen years between herself and her youngest sister, when her mother Alice died, Vi again scooped up her family, taking in little Martha and bringing her up alongside her own children. Of course, this needed financing, and so, on top of her day job as a cotton weaver, Vi worked in the evening as an usherette in the town's cinema, where she sold ice cream for a ha'penny. My mother often recalled that is what they did in those days and laughed when remembering Violet's favourite saying, that 'there was only one woman ever stuck fast and they pulled her through with the help of God and two policemen'. With wartime rationing, the little food they had was shared and there was always room for family, even in the smallest of houses. The 1921 census revealed how, as young folk themselves, my grandparents lived in two and three bedroomed terraced houses – eight occupants in each. Not surprising then that throughout her life, much to the frustration of her own children, my mother had no concept of what we would now call personal space. When little Martha came to live with them, our Rosie had no choice but to budge up and they shared a single bed, top-to-toe, until her wedding day. As a mother, she expected her own children to 'make a do', share and accommodate others, because that is what families do. We 'get on with it' because 'that is how it is'. When my father, her husband of sixty-five years, was taken into hospital, she said it was the first time she had slept alone.

A Lancashire back street

Chapter 4

She is so joyous and fresh, so light of heart and free of spirit, and so guileless and unsuspecting too – Oh, it would be cruel to make her feel as I feel now, and know what I have known![16]

Down the years, I came to understand my tribe, who I was and where I had come from. Around the kitchen table, warmed, and fed by a coal-fuelled stove, I listened to my mother's endless stories. Balanced on a little twig that was my place in the family tree, I was secure. And yet there was an unsettled stirring too. Disguised as laughter, there was always a tinge of bluntness in my mother's anecdotes … the grounding reality that life is hard, and we have no right to expect it to be otherwise. Her words of wisdom were endless: say your prayers, count your blessings and always be kind. But as a girl growing up in the 1970s, I was bewildered. I did not see a world of gratitude or kindness in my mother's stories, only a harsh struggle for survival. Violet's assault on her father was not the only story of women being forced to defend themselves against vile men. Oh, how my mother laughed when she spoke of another clay-pipe smoking matriarch. On dark nights, great-grandma Sara Ellen O'Leary carried an iron poker under her shawl as a weapon of self-defence. A younger self pondered how strong women, with hearts and hearths big enough to hold life and death, dwelt in dark places too. Were my grandmothers and great-grandmothers gutsy women who learned to look after themselves and each other, or were they dangerous, poker-carrying delinquents? What did that make me? What did life have in store, and how could I ever live up to their legendary courage?

Reflecting on those times and my mother's storytelling, I wonder if these tales were parables, woven and embellished to convey a secret message to innocent young girls. Family folklore was infused with hidden metaphors and characterised by never quite getting to the point, thus creating space for curiosity and fear. In the 1970s, I knew nothing about sex except for puzzling snippets of information from giggling girls in the schoolyard. And yet, I knew that there were some men, a local clergyman especially, who frightened me. The fixed stare of his reptilian eyes, peering through a thick, jam-jar lens of black-framed spectacles lingered too long. The rancid, sweaty smell of his black clothes and flaked, greasy hair preceded his arrival in the classroom and hung around long after he had gone. One day I went to school with a hole in my knickers, and he laughed and shamed me in front of my friends. I was eight years old, and the knickers were red.

These creeps as we called them disgusted and confused. They kept secrets. They came too close. Some things were never spoken of in our house, but I know now that my mother's stories were veiled warnings that there was something out there to be afraid of. Surround yourself with women you can trust and beware of men, seemed to be the message. As well as not knowing what I should be afraid of or why, I absorbed the steely, cruel, bitchy undercurrent of shame and silence that seemed to be part and parcel of being a girl – 'say nowt … least said soonest mended'. Should bad things happen, the woman was always to blame. In overhearing gossip about 'silly lasses' who went to Blackpool and came home pregnant, I learned that judgment was harsh. Womenfolk may well be there to cover up the mess but one mistake and a girl's standing in her family and community was tarnished forever. Most times, no words or explanation were needed, the knowing looks and sinister vibes were enough. I may have had no idea of where babies came from, but I knew that for some girls there was stigma and blame. Silly girls should never go to Blackpool, and I should never have invited shame by going to school with a hole in my knickers. The fear of *something*, of not knowing what or why, a dark *something*, was engrained in the psyche of so many little girls in those days. Some may say the demon that was shame lingered into adult life.

Tangled in the thorny, complex world of men, my mother also remembered kindness, comfort and security, especially from her dear old dad. 'I have never known a time when I have not felt loved' she would often say. In her memories of childhood, she recalled loving uncles who rallied and supported when times were hard. Uncle Ernie was a chauffeur for a posh family of mill owners in the town. On the rare occasions he was allowed to take the car for the day, he would fill it with hungry kids and take them for a spin and a picnic over the hills and far away to Haworth or the Yorkshire Dales. Then there was Uncle Cyril, who lost his hearing in the war. All his life, he carried two hearing aids the size of cigarette packets in his waistcoat pocket. He loved Blackpool, and in the summer would take little Rosie for a train ride and a day on the sands. It was there he met his girlfriend Winnie and courted her for twenty years.

Then there was my saintly father. Our Frank. Childhood sweethearts and the love of her life, my parents knew each other all their lives and were married for sixty-five years. As influenced by youth culture as kids are today, my parents loved the cinema, especially the Hollywood musicals of the 1940s and 50s. Believers in true love, theirs was a Doris Day and Judy Garland philosophy of life; in other words, work hard, live well and 'direct your feet to the sunny side of the street'. Although my mother would rant and complain about his shortcomings and annoying habits, in truth, there was no man like our Frank. My quest in life was to be good enough, to find true love just like her and to find a man as flawless as my godly father. For a shy, sensitive, spotty and undeserving girl, this was an impossible task. With bogeymen to the left of me, saints to the right, there I was, stuck in the middle … Confused.

In a man's world, the Brontë sisters first published under the male pseudonyms of Currer, Ellis and Acton Bell. *Jane Eyre*, *Wuthering Heights* and *Agnes Grey* were all published in 1847, with *The Tenant of Wildfell Hall*, Anne's second novel, following in 1848. All were received with shock reviews whilst simultaneously being lapped up by a population hungry for tales of female resilience, male sexual immorality, drink, debauchery, and in the end, redemption, reconciliation and true love. With brazen, uncomfortable truths, these novels made awkward reading for many. Almost two hundred years later, they continue to challenge the reader to face the broken, nasty side of humanity and hear the voice of women. With an innate, northern intolerance of hypocrisy and dry cynical humour, the Brontë sisters refused to 'suffer fools gladly', and that is why my mother loved them. They were like her and all the women she knew. It was not as if the sisters did not struggle with the morality of their writing, but with grit and determination, they had the courage of their convictions. Homes *were* violent and cruel. People *were* poor. Women *were* oppressed.

Without apology, in defence of *The Tenant of Wildfell Hall*, Anne Brontë explained how she was driven by moral duty to tell the truth. As a young governess, no more than a child herself, Anne had witnessed the tumultuous lives of the middle classes. As a sister, she lived alongside her brother Branwell as he fell into a spiral of addiction. Charlotte wrote to a friend, 'so long as he remains at home I scarce dare hope for peace in the house ... in his present state it is scarcely possible to stay in the room where he is'.[17] For Anne, the experience of living with a broken Branwell fed her creativity and drive to speak the truth, as it became the twisted, life and death character of Arthur Huntingdon in *The Tenant of Wildfell Hall*.

As daughters of the Reverend Patrick Brontë, Charlotte, Emily and Anne were at the heart of the Christian community in Haworth. Their writing pours out godly wisdom and biblical quotes by the dozen, whilst at the same time inviting a cynical contempt and questioning of the status quo. Growing up in a Catholic world, hellfire and damnation was a dominating feature in my mother's life too – and arguably, not far removed from the Brontës' experience. Christian teaching and the lived reality of the harsh, cruel world of good Christian folk was a paradox I could not work out. It never sat comfortably, and I sense that was their struggle too. Likewise, the domineering misogynist as rescuer and hero also presented a conundrum. Ultimately, the Brontë novels are powerful love stories in which true love is forever on the terms of their women characters: Catherine Earnshaw, Jane Eyre, Helen Graham, Agnes Grey, Lucy Snowe and Shirley Keedler. Upholding ethics of truth, courage and self-belief, these fictitious women called out abuse and transformed the dark, shadow side of the men they loved. It was thus with the womenfolk in my mother's world. There was forever a sobering reality that life was as it was. Women knew their place in a world of men. Although they may have imagined it otherwise, poverty and religion kept them where they were, and so they had no choice but to make the most of it and play by their own clandestine rules. The unbreakable bond of women, characterised by a strong backbone, warm heart and cynical humour were the tools of survival. Stick to your guns, stand by your man and never, ever give in.

Chapter 5

I say, there were giants on the earth in those days: giants that strove to scale heaven. The first woman's breast that heaved with life on this world yielded the daring which could contend with Omnipotence: the strength which could bear a thousand years of bondage.[18]

Such was the sense of community and the oral tradition of an Irish heritage, the women of my family were at their happiest together, sitting around the coal fire, reading, gossiping, sharing stories and having a laugh at the expense of their menfolk. To say that my mother had an anecdote for every occasion is an understatement. What is more, she was a woman of truth. *Her* truth. When she made her mind up about something, it became fact. For example, fussy eaters were cautioned that if you don't eat your supper, your stomach would digest itself in the night, and girls who used tampons were damaged forever. Whatever had happened in my life, she always had some tale or words of wisdom to offer, drawing on her passion for all things Brontë to embellish the point. My mother considered them kinfolk and shared their strong, unbending sense of place and of home. After all, they had lived just over the hill, and being of Irish descent, we were practically related. Obviously. The view from our window was towards the landscape the Brontë family called home. The panorama from the moor that was their playground and inspiration mirrored back towards the witching country of Pendle Hill and to us.

Haworth and the Brontës were hers and, by osmosis, ours. No coincidence was lost on my mother. Charlotte, Emily and Anne, a trinity of sisters. Our Rosie was one of three sisters, and she had three daughters. For some reason, this was a sign. She would often muse what life was really like for the sisters of Haworth who lived, slept and wrote together. How much of their experiences reflected her own? Working-class women with backbone shared the strong work ethic of the Brontë sisters, who had no choice but to 'learn to stand on their own two feet'. Proud and dignified, did these hard-working women dream of fame or, like her, were they simply trying to make their way through life in the best way they knew how? Did they share a secret pact as they had done in their childhood world? What did they say to each other as they sat around their dining table, writing by candlelight? What made them laugh? Did they fall out and argue like sisters so often do? Theories of sibling rivalry are rife in the myths and analysis that have grown up around the Brontës over the years. My mother would scoff, that there was no mystery, nothing to see here, only the reality of family life. Emily was big sister Charlotte's 'bonnie love'. Of Emily's illness, Charlotte wrote,

> When she is ill there seems to be no sunshine in the world for me; the tie of sisters is near and dear indeed, and I think a certain harshness in her powerful, and peculiar character only makes me cling to her more.[19]

No doubt they were brutally honest with each other in a way only sisters can be, yet there was total acceptance and an unbreakable bond of loyalty, truth, friendship and ardent sister love.

But the parallels didn't end there. To constant amusement, my mother even found similarities between herself and Charlotte, both being women of petite stature. Charlotte Brontë was a dainty little woman, described by Elizabeth Gaskell as having 'hands and feet the smallest I ever saw; when one of the former was placed in mine, it was like the soft touch of a bird in the middle of my palm'.[20] On one occasion, when discussing the display of Charlotte's dainty shoes in the Brontë Parsonage Museum, my mother joked how they would have been a perfect fit, at which point my father chimed in, 'but not the waistline'. He was promptly slapped on the arm with a rolled-up newspaper. Charlotte, the girl who had beaten the odds and became the writer she wanted to be was my mother's heroine. Equally, *Jane Eyre* was her bible for little women, a timeless handbook on how to stand up for oneself, to stand one's ground and to be heard. A favourite Rosie quote echoed Jane's impassioned declaration to Mr Rochester: 'do you think, because I am poor, obscure, plain and little, I am soulless and heartless? You think wrong!'.[21] In other words, I may be little, I may be a woman but don't dare mess with me!

For over fifty years, my father ran a carpentry business. He was a hands-on grafter who believed that 'a hard day's work never hurt anyone'. My mother, the organiser behind the operation, managed phone calls, ran the accounts and paid the wages each week for a dozen men. This meant that every Thursday, rain or shine, she tootled off to catch the bus to the bank with a battered tartan shopping bag on her arm. Wearing a red tartan wool coat complemented by a matching tam o'shanter, she meant business. It was the 70s after all. A huge bundle of brown and blue bank notes, bags of shiny coins and copper were deposited in the tartan receptacle, and she then proceeded to cart it home on the bus. At no point did it occur to our Rosie that she was at risk, for this tiny lady knew that she was the offspring of poker-carrying warriors, women who knew how to look after themselves in an unpredictable world. Bringing home the booty, my mother would empty the bag on the kitchen table and carefully count out the money, placing the correct wage into brown envelopes – one for each man.

When my mother was working, she was not to be disturbed. Sitting quietly, nervously playing behind the sofa, I was surprised one day when she beckoned me. It was February 1971. Pulling up a chair, she allowed me to sit with her. 'Look,' she said, tipping out bags of bright, shiny copper and silver coins onto the table. 'This is new money. It is called decimalisation. See,' she counted, 'two halfpennies make one penny, ten pennies are the same as one ten pence piece, ten of these make one pound' … and so it went on. Not one to trust the newfangled invention of the pocket calculator, all sums were worked out in her head and on paper. Each year, the accounts were audited by an austere and rather smelly gentleman called Mr Temple. Like her mother before her, Rosie believed that keeping men well fed was key to a peaceful life. Sitting at our kitchen table, with crumbs of homemade cake in his straggled beard, Mr Temple would congratulate my mother on her exemplary business and baking acumen.

My mother often described herself as a 'home bird'. In other words, she loved being at home surrounded by what was familiar and would often say, 'the world comes to me'. For her, there could never be enough children around the place; our house was always open and welcoming to uncles, aunties, nephews, nieces, cousins, neighbours and friends. A permanent fixture on the kitchen table was a decrepit old biscuit tin, which was a wedding present and souvenir from the Queen's Coronation in 1953. It brimmed with a seemingly endless supply of homemade jammy buns and the kettle was always on, even for strangers. In our town, there was a homeless man called Norman. In those days, everyone knew him and looked out for his welfare. My mother remembered him fondly and recalled how one night he knocked at our door and asked if he could sleep in the outhouse. My mother said, 'of course!' and made him a pint pot of hot tea and a sandwich. The next morning, she made him breakfast and he went on his way, with cheese butties wrapped in paper and a pocket full of jammy buns.

As in family life, so in business. A signal that trouble was brewing was my mother metaphorically firing a warning shot across the bows by quoting Shakespeare, 'though she be but little she is fierce'. As well as the accountant, our Rosie's other role in the business was the designated driver. In a clapped-out, long wheelbase Land Rover, she would do her rounds, twice a day. For donkey's years, at half-past seven each morning, she would meet the employees at an allocated pick-up point at the top of town, drop them off at their place of work for the day and reverse the trip every evening. In between, of course, she had the school run, a home and business to manage, meals to cook and an ailing mother to care for. Throughout that time, my younger self took all this for granted. When my mother told us she knew nothing, that her life was ordinary, it never occurred to me to question her truth. I quite simply believed her. Only in later years, as a mother myself, I began to understand and really appreciate this intelligent, able, resilient woman and the many roles, responsibilities, joys and heartaches she juggled with every day of her life. It must have been exhausting – and boring. Although she ranted and complained most days, in her failing years, in her writing and storytelling, she recalled that she never imagined or wished for a different life. Some of the men who worked with my father attended his funeral, and a year later, my mother's too. Over a pie and pint in the pub afterwards, they reminisced about those days (some fifty years ago) and roared with laughter when one of them said how he had loved my mother to bits – but that all the lads were scared stiff of her.

Throughout her life and spilling into her own diaries, our Rosie often spoke of how every day there was baking on the go, five pounds of potatoes to be peeled and a loaf of bread to be sliced and buttered. The few surviving letters and diary papers penned by Emily Brontë offer insight into everyday life at the Parsonage and, in particular, the goings-on in the kitchen. In a diary paper dated 24 November 1834, she writes,

Taby said just now come Anne pillopatate (ie pill a potato)
We are going to have for Dinner Boiled BeefTurnips, potato's
and applepudding the Kitchin is in avery untidy state.[22]

Eleven years later, in a diary paper dated 31 July 1845, spuds and
housework are still on her mind,

Tabby has just been teasing me to turn as formerly to
'pilloputate' – Anne and I should have picked the black
currants if it had been fine and sunshiny – I must hurry off
now to my turning and ironing I have plenty of work on hands
and writing and am altogether full of business.[23]

As a child, and even now as a motherless daughter, I remember
my mother's 'pilloputate' hands: tiny, cold and wet, with serrated
fingernails blackened with soil. And the daily panic to 'get the tea
on' before rushing to her next task. At the onset of her forgetfulness,
our Rosie's diaries evoked memories of her younger self, a hard-
working, strong, feisty whirlwind of a woman, with a giant's heart,
loving, warm, cuddly, always there and always the same.

In the mist of fading frailty, the stories I had heard thousands
of times were strangely comforting, evoking my own memories
of how, for a little girl, at the end each of terrifying, nun-infested
school day, there was always the safe place of hearth, home and my
mother's storytelling. Dad was a sportsman, and like many working-
class men of the time, spent his evenings in the pub playing darts
and weekends watching football, cricket or playing golf. I didn't
miss him because that is what dads did in those days. Besides, this
was girl's stuff and not a place of interest to my father. Moreover, it
meant that after tearing around all day, serving others, my mother
was at last there, for and with her children. In those precious times,

if we weren't reading books, we were sharing stories, anecdotes from the day, whopping tales of schoolyard combat or playful banter.

Being alongside, listening to chit-chat and family sagas from long ago, rooted me in a deep sense of belonging. In a shared feminine space, occupied by ancestors, friends, community and of course, the Brontës, I was home. Here, women were flawed, complex and hard-working. They had backbone, courage and intelligence. In this place of being and belonging, the first fragile shoots of who I was and the hopes and dreams of who I might become, began to gently emerge. In my acute shyness, I wanted to read books forever, to absorb repeatedly the words of Jane Eyre: 'I am no bird; and no net ensnares me; I am a free human being with an independent will, which I now exert to leave you'.[24] I wanted to be a writer too and to fly the nest, but being very much my mother's daughter, at that time I had no sense of self-worth or faith that I had any ability whatsoever. When I came to having my first book published, my mother was, in the moment, thrilled; but after a few minutes, she had no recollection of the news. 'Such is life!' she would have said.

I remember my mother's 'pillopatate' hands

Chapter 6

why, he was as he was ... I cannot tell: it is a deep mystery.
The key is in the hands of his Maker: there I leave it.[25]

On her trips down memory lane, my mother would often say, 'we didn't know we were poor'. Owning a book in the 1930s was a rarity for a poor lass and only a dolly daydream would entertain the fantasy of writing one. Young Rosalie O'Riley had the luxury of owning two books: *Wuthering Heights* and *Jane Eyre*. I do not know what happened to the latter but still have my mother's copy of *Wuthering Heights*. How it came to her is a mystery, but it was one of her few material treasures. The title, now faded black with age, is obscured on the red, hardback cover and fine, yellowed threads cling to a wobbly, sewn spine. Speckles of brown, peppered pages and my mother's inscription of her name, proudly written in ink copperplate hand, offers a clue to a family artefact. This book, intact and legible, is at least eighty years old. It has woven its magic across three generations and inspired what I have come to call the Brontë barometer on men; for my mother was adamant that the sisters were familiar with the traits of all the male characters in their books and that they grew out of lived experience.

An alternative caption for this chapter could have been taken from the novel *Shirley*, in which Charlotte Brontë introduced a section with the heading, 'Which the genteel reader is recommended to skip, low persons being here introduced'.[26] In the same way our Rosie had, throughout her life encountered toxic men with nasty tempers, Charlotte, Emily and Anne had their share of personal troubles, not least with brother Branwell. These days, he would be described as having alcohol and addiction issues at the very least; but in my mother's language and life experience, Branwell was simply hopeless and could not cope with the fact that he had three clever sisters. Grounded in northern landscapes, language and culture, the Brontës spoke to working-class readers in the mill towns of Lancashire and Yorkshire. Throughout her life, my mother upheld the assertion that the world is full of real-life versions of the characters they created – Heathcliffs, Haretons, Huntingdons, Rochesters and all kinds of personalities in between. Not a lot had changed in the lives of the peculiar folk who inhabited the hillsides and valleys across the moor, and she would regularly say, 'we ain't got money but we do see life'.

Referring to Emily Brontë's creation in *Wuthering Heights*, one of my mother's archetypes was the character of Heathcliff, the manipulative, controlling abuser, with power to create fear in the minds of all he encountered. With cruelty and evil ascribed to him, Heathcliff is of the uncanny, described by Brontë as 'a fierce, pitiless, wolfish man' with 'sharp cannibal teeth' and 'basilisk eyes.' 'He is a lying fiend, a monster and not a human being', 'a goblin, a ghoul or a vampire, a hideous incarnate demon'.[27] For me, these chilling attributes serve to reinforce the power of a character never to be underestimated, and Emily's absolute genius in birthing this creature in human form. More simply, in our Rosie's world, Heathcliff conjured up the image of a domineering bully or a man with outrageous, disgusting, habits and unpredictable behaviour. It also applied in general to all grumpy men in a strop, or those with strange habits that included a lack of personal hygiene. 'Ignore him; he is doing a Heathcliff', was her motherly advice when any cantankerous old sod crossed our path.

When I was thirteen, in 1976, the family emigrated, or so it seemed. Horror of horrors, we moved to a farmhouse twenty miles away. Deeper into the untamed, sweeping hills, our neighbour was a grumpy farmer with feral children who, with their father's gun, would often be seen hunting for rabbits and shooting rats. If they happened on us, they would threaten to shoot us too. Had this occurred in the here and now, these incidents would be of concern to Social Services and may even have made national news; but it was a time when, with a shrug, we were reassured that there were some funny folk on that hillside, and it was ever thus. 'It's like living next door to Heathcliff,' my mother would bluster dramatically with her usual sweeping judgement.

Waking from a dream, forty years on, one of Rosie's diary entries, written in capital letters and with a shaky hand, read, 'stark naked man'. Enquiring what on earth she meant evoked a chuckle and another memory of that time. Returning home from walking the dog, I found my mother in a screeching panic. A neighbour had telephoned to say that a man in a pink suit had been spotted lurking around the farm buildings near our house. As a young teenager, I was mortified to learn that this man was in fact naked. He was a streaker, another strange manifestation on the hillside, further proving my mother's assertion, like Mrs Gaskell before her, that isolation fostered unwholesome behaviour.[28] Over the years, my mother would often refer to this 'to-do' and men in pink suits became a metaphor and veiled warning to beware of funny fellas and daft 'apeths clowning around.

On the hillside of the weird, fully suited and booted was Farmer Clegg and his three-legged dog Finn. Another gun-carrying, rabbit hunter, he would hurl the dead prey over his shoulder and stomp across the swampy fields to check his fishing lines in the nearby river. He would nod and touch the edge of his flat cap to acknowledge my mother. Because of this, he was judged as being odd but acceptable, despite the unsavoury habit of storing meat pies in the bonnet of his truck to keep them warm. On the occasions he did speak, it was in the broad dialect, unique to that part of the world, made timeless by the character of the grumpy, goblin-like Joseph in *Wuthering Heights*. The manservant and observer of the 'queer goings-on' at the Heights, Joseph is a hater of women, describing Catherine Earnshaw as 'yah gooid fur nowt, slatternly witch'. Detesting strangers and damning outsiders of all kinds he commands, 'na-ay! yah muh goa back to whear yah coom frough'.[29] Oh, how my mother would laugh when academics and offcumdens debated the mysterious quandary of Emily Brontë's rationale in creating such an enigmatic being. Joseph's language rolled off the tongue in our part of the world and his character and colloquialisms lived on in our house and community. In her frailty and in her diaries, Rosie would often recall her first date, when she went 'a coorting'.[30] Her father had opened the door to dear Frank with the words, 'what dos't tha want?'.

In our world, toys were 'lakins', playthings. How she giggled when I reminded her of the occasion, many years later, when I bumped into Farmer Clegg and stopped to say hello. When I mentioned I was buying a house, he asked, 'art lakin' at being wed?'. No, it was just me. 'Nah, then then,' said he in surprise, 'all t' best' and in touching the brim of his flat cap, acknowledged his respect and best wishes to my mother. I have never seen him since. *Wuthering Heights* was published in 1847 to poor reviews, not least for its coarse and vulgar characters. 'Well, there you have it,' my mother would say. 'I rest my case.' Resting her case, in a personal letter to a friend, Charlotte explained:

The puzzle is that while the people in the South object to my delineation of Northern life and manners, the people of Yorkshire and Lancashire approve: they say it is precisely that contrast of rough nature with highly artificial cultivation which forms one of their main characteristics; … the question arises whether do the London Critics or the old Northern Squires understand the matter best?[31]

The final straw that led to us upping sticks and flitting back to whence we came, was a phone call from the police requesting that they use our house for surveillance. There was a suspicion of criminal activity in the area and our shifty neighbours were people of interest. With my father at work and the kids at school, my mother spent a terrifying day alone at home, with armed police in the house, garden and surrounding undergrowth, waiting for God knows what. The commotion came to nothing, and she was furious. With her fierce mother love and instinct to protect her young once again kicking in, the police got a stern telling off, and what is more, my little mamma, five foot in stature, with a giant of a temper, tore a strip off the neighbours. She had no care for who they were or what they were up to, but they were not going to do it on her doorstep – and that was final. The scary, hairy, shifty neighbour could not have been more contrite, and normal life was resumed. However, the thing that upset my mother most was not that they were potential inhabitants of the criminal underworld but that they left their washing on the line for days on end. And there were never any knickers pegged out. Living next door to the fur coat and no knickers brigade was simply not on. It was inconceivable to continue to bring up her daughters next door to such mucky folk. And so off we trekked, back over the hills and dales to resume life in the shadow of Boulsworth moor. Of course, over the years, my mother's storytelling enhanced these tales of tempestuous interludes and disturbed hillside dwellers. As night follows day, the conversation would always shift to our Rosie's philosophy that 'there's nowt n'funnier than folk', that the Brontës knew best and that for every toxic man, there is an enabling woman, who on no account should take any messing from them buggers.

There was no doubt in my mother's mind that, like her, the Brontë sisters too suffered alongside the eccentric and unconventional and wrote them into some of the greatest works of English literature. Mrs Gaskell would seem to support this theory, describing the powerful force of character among the 'dwellers in the lonely houses far away in upland districts', and cautioning that 'a solitary life cherishes mere fancies until they become manias'.[32] Eliciting local folklore, Gaskell wrote of a vicar who horsewhipped non-church attendees and a local squire, drunk as a lord, who ordered a cockfighting pit to be set up in his bedchamber so he could have one last gamble on his deathbed. Both these accounts of local goings-on were also part of my mother's repertoire; but in her case, the vicar was a local Catholic priest, and my great grandfather was one of those on the receiving end, not of a horsewhip but of an Irishman's shillelagh.

Going on to explain how 'the people of Haworth were no less strong and full of character than their neighbours on either side of the hill',[33] Gaskell was uncomfortable with how the Brontë sisters analysed and harnessed these ruffians and their crude characteristics in their novels, almost begging the forgiveness and understanding of the reader. It was as if she excused their choices because they were poor, isolated and had a hard life, as if they knew no better. Our Rosie begged to differ. Encouraged by their parents to be curious, literature, poetry and politics stoked the young, inquisitive minds of the Brontë children. Life *was* hard, they *were* poor and in many ways, isolated, but imagination, combined with genius and honesty, knows no boundaries.

It is easy to forget that parents are people too and had lives before children. Patrick and Maria Brontë had extraordinary lives before their marriage. With Irish roots, Patrick forged a path out of extreme poverty to become a Cambridge graduate and an author in his own right. As a middle-class young lady from Cornwall, Maria Brontë wrote poetry. Like my mother, it is easy to imagine Patrick and Maria as parents who filled their home with stories of faraway people and places. My imagination teases, as I wonder if the sisters drew on their parents' tales and secretly folded them into their own stories. As a child, I was hungry to hear stories of kinfolk and faraway places, and as youngsters do, would beg for tales to be told repeatedly. Did the Brontë children do the same? In Anne Brontë's *Agnes Grey*, the fortunes of the family were lost in a shipwreck. One can only imagine that this is rooted in family myth, as Maria Brontë did indeed lose most of her belongings in a shipwreck off the Cornish coast.[34] How exotic and exciting a tale this must have been for those motherless children. It is moving to imagine that Anne hid a little bit of her mother in her first novel as a silent hug and gentle nod to a parent she barely remembered.

Poor Emily did not live to see the reviews of *Wuthering Heights*. Accused of being a book with no moral compass, it was a shocking, crude and distasteful tale. In contrast to Anne's resolve to voice the truth in her novels, in writing the preface to the second edition of *Wuthering Heights*, a grieving Charlotte apologetically explained its quality as, 'moorish, and wild, and knotty as a root of heath'.[35] One can only imagine the early days of raw bereavement. Exhausted, depressed and with pain in her heart, Charlotte was driven by big sister instinct to limit the damage and to protect her younger sibling from the backlash of the monster she had created. A grieving Charlotte queried if it was right or advisable for Emily to have created a being like Heathcliff and to unleash him on the world.

Unlike Mary Shelley's Frankenstein, Heathcliff was human, and this is what made *Wuthering Heights* so shocking. His disturbing, cruel and dysfunctional characteristics demonstrate the worst of the dark and frightening side of human behaviour.

Alongside Heathcliff, and having read *Wuthering Heights* countless times, my skin still crawls at the repulsive character of Hareton 'slavering into a jug' and hanging puppies from the back of a chair for fun.[36] This poor child, a victim of domestic violence in the extreme, is a harrowing image. Emily, in her genius and innocence, told her story without apology. She could do no other, for that is who she was. Her big sister's bonnie love, Emily was a girl of unbending spirit, for whom 'an interpreter ought always to have stood between her and the world'.[37] When positive reviews of *Wuthering Heights* were eventually published, Charlotte was both grateful that her sister's genius had at last been appreciated and saddened that it had taken so long. 'The masterpiece of a poet … we are at a loss to find anywhere in modern prose … such wealth … such apparent ease, such instinctive art'.[38] Like so many ordinary folks before her, my mother was enriched by her love of Emily Brontë and interpreted her life and work for herself, within the context of her own understanding. She shared Emily's love of landscape and home until her closing breath, and the meaning she assigned to her characters, kept Rosalie's imagination alive until her last days.

Chapter 7

**And you will have such nice rambles on the moors! ... you
can bring a book in fine weather, and make a green hollow
your study.**[39]

On sprawling barren hillsides, tumbling ruins of stone barns
and farmhouses cleave to the boggy earth. These scenes on the
edge of Patrick Brontë's parish were as much part of the backdrop
to my childhood as purple heather in late summer and snowdrifts in
winter. The stories and characters woven into the ancient landscape
were alive with love, passion and raw humanity. What the Brontë
sisters imagined was real to me, in my blood, under my skin. To my
mother, they were, quite simply, family. Written from her bed in
the last two years of life, our Rosie's diaries reveal the importance of
this connection, as she repeatedly wrote how, enjoying her first taste
of independence at the age of fourteen, she got the bus to Haworth
with a friend: 'Marion Turner introduced me to the Brontës. Bus
ride via Keighley. I have had great enjoyment from reading their
books and their lives'. For the working classes of the mill towns,
holidays (or 'th'olidies' as my mother would say) meant a day out.
Choosing a trip to Haworth over a train ride to Blackpool Tower is
a heartwarming insight into an old lady's teenage passion.

Now, it may be true that my mother, like Mrs Gaskell and many
other enthusiasts before her, was responsible for creating her own
Brontë myth. The story goes that Charlotte's second marriage

proposal, so wisely rejected, was from the curate who resided at the church around the corner from where we lived. Rosie's theory was reinforced by a conversation she had with a plumber who came to install central heating in our house in 1975. He had been renovating a farmhouse a short distance from the church. It had been lived in by an old lady and had never been touched in donkey's years. On clearing out the kitchen, at the back of a drawer, he found an original drawing, a sketch of Charlotte Brontë. What happened to it, we never knew, but ever since, without fail, every time my mother walked past the blackened church, with its grim gravestones, she wondered about that drawing. Who put it there, who was the artist, what became of it? Did the Brontës walk these familiar paths? A convoluted connection or wild fantasy perhaps. Yet the story of Charlotte's portrait reverberated in my mother's storytelling over the years and was repeated in her diary and memory until her last days.

Nestled at the foot of Boulsworth moor is the hamlet of Wycoller, an ancient settlement layered in myth and legend. Burrowed in an isolated valley, this is the heart of God's country. Protected and bordered by archaic stone posts, there is one labyrinthine, moss-shrouded, slippery road in and out. Archaeological discoveries of flint tools and axes suggest that the area has been inhabited for 3,000 years or more. Later, sheep farming led to a woollen trade cottage industry, but as mill towns grew and chimneys popped up like mushrooms among the hills and valleys of Lancashire and Yorkshire, the homespun industry collapsed. Families had no choice but to move to local towns. And so, as if under a witch's spell, Wycoller was abandoned and slept for hundreds of years.

As kids, we would walk to Wycoller, sometimes ghost hunting with a bunch of friends, but more often than not, with our Uncle Tony. This was a man who could swear like a trooper and would give us sixpence to do the same. But underneath the loud and gruff exterior, he was a kind, caring and gentle soul, who always had time for his nieces and nephews. With a picnic of boiled ham butties wrapped in brown paper, a packet of biscuits and orange squash in a used, glass pop bottle, he would stride out like the Pied Piper, with a trail of dishevelled kids behind him. Keeping up and no complaining were the rules of these epic hikes. It was hard for a small girl with little legs, but I was determined to keep up with the gang and trotted along happily.

Scrambling over the mossy wreckage of walls and the stone lintels of windows and doors, the ruin of Wycoller Hall was our playground. We would build dams in the beck by the ancient Packhorse Bridge and climb the rocks of Foster's Leap, a rocky outcrop where, legend has it, the last owner of Wycoller Hall fell to his death. This late 18th-century character was a drunk, gambler and all-round bad 'un who came out of the wrong end of a bet when he attempted to jump across the crevasses in the rocks on his horse. He was fatally injured, as was the horse, poor thing. It would not take a leap of imagination to link this local story to the *Wuthering Heights* character of Hindley Earnshaw, the drunken brother of Cathy and arch-enemy of Heathcliff, who 'died true to his character, drunk as a lord'.[40] I also took a tumble at Foster's Leap, when I lost a shoe in a muddy pothole. Although the end of the world to me, it brought no attention or sympathy, only a roar of hearty laughter and a loud expletive from Uncle Tony – who had to retrieve the stinking object from the slimy mess.

A mill worker and weaver by day, Uncle Tony was a great storyteller, a spinner of yarns. Huddled together on the cold stone seat of the ancient fireplace, strangely still standing among the shambles of Wycoller Hall, Uncle Tony would tell us how Charlotte Brontë probably came to this very place and how we were sitting in the spot that was Ferndean Manor in *Jane Eyre*. Of the moors around

Wuthering Heights, Emily wrote how 'the place was haunted ... swarming with ghosts and goblins'.[41] In a similar manner, Uncle Tony told tales of ancient druids who had dwelt in this valley, the Clam Bridge, believed to be over a thousand years old, and the ghosts of a Blue Lady and a Headless Horseman. Hands reaching towards my face, with fingers wriggling in a ghoulish pose, he would tease, 'It is said that in the darkness you can hear the blood-curdling screams of victims of horrible deaths and murder.' On a roll, he would talk of the trial of the Pendle Witches and the curse of Alizon Device who, not a stone's throw away, cast a spell that killed a local peddler. This sparked one of the darkest and most cruel chapters in 17th-century England – the persecution and trial of the Lancashire witches. 'Beware of the dark,' he would taunt. 'The ghost of Heathcliff walks'.

On one occasion, we heard a blood-curdling scream coming from the woodland path known as Wycoller Dene, the route of the Headless Horseman. Clinging to Uncle Tony, it was no comfort to find out that the shriek was my older sister, who was being chased, not by a ghost – but a goat. His hearty laugh boomed and echoed around the shell of the haunted Hall. This event, like so many others over time, was exaggerated, embroidered and woven into family oral tradition. Entertaining, frightening and grim in equal measure, these tales, old and new, have been passed through generations. How many of Uncle Tony's tall stories were myth and how many were true, I have no clue – but it matters not. All were enmeshed together to create a unique family folklore, where my roots are buried. That is the purpose of them, to imprint and stir the magic of belonging and place.

In *Wuthering Heights*, little Cathy asks, 'how long will it be before I can walk to the top of those hills? What lies on the other side – is it the sea?'[42] I ponder if Emily asked her own father the same question.

One of Uncle Tony's fables was that on a clear day you could see the Irish Sea from the top of Boulsworth Hill. But in truth, there never was a day sunny enough. Maybe it was another one of his tall tales, shared with the purpose of awakening curiosity and dreams. Somewhere, over there, adventure was to be had. And he grasped the dream, my Uncle Tony, thus bringing another hefty blow to my small world. When wooden crates were delivered to our door on a dark winter's evening, I learned that he had gone to live far away. I have no memory of goodbyes, just an acceptance of a new reality and a childlike pride in his courage. His role in giving me a sense of roots and belonging was balanced with new adventures, as Uncle Tony's epic letters brought to life tales of his new world, Australia. With gifts of toys and books, we learned about the Blue Mountains and the Bush, the people of the land, and of strange animals, such as wombats, kangaroos and sleeping koalas, curled like toys on eucalyptus sticks.

For five generations, Wycoller has been cherished by grandparents, great-grandparents, parents and now my own children, who have trodden gingerly across the stony bridges, picnicked in the ruins of the tumbledown Hall and paddled in the clear, ice-cold water of the bonnie beck. For my mother, Wycoller was hallowed turf, sacred to the Brontës. So often, she ruminated if Charlotte, Branwell, Emily and Anne clambered over the same bridges and walls, as they played their childhood games of Angria and Gondal. Did their wooden pattens, like the wooden clogs of our Rosie's childhood, clatter in the hollows of the stone-flagged floor of the Hall? Sitting where we sat over 150 years later, did they huddle together in the ruin of the stone fireplace and conjure up their characters? Did Charlotte imagine the fireside scenes – Mr Rochester's chair, his opaque, injured eyes gazing into the flames, dreaming, calling out to Jane Eyre across the void? At their feet, did Keeper and Flossy, their beloved pets, play, igniting the imagining of Pilot the dog, the faithful guardian of his owner Mr Rochester? Did they visualise the Hall in its heyday, panelled with tapestried wall hangings made from the wool of local sheep? My mother's answer to all these musings was of course a resounding yes! Our Rosie never lost her enthusiasm for the wonderings and wanderings of Wycoller and the Brontës. Over and over, these same discussions brought her joy and the sense of knowing that she was home. Layered with fantasy, as frailty and forgetfulness closed in, the energy of the place, echoed in her memory.

Clam Bridge Wycoller

Over strangely still standing water of the bonny beck
death eyes green hollowed ruins,
sacred shambles of the tumbledown Hall.
Ghosts of memory, their tapestried musings
guard forgetful wanderings of nestled laughter.
Mill workers walk these familiar paths and
cast a spell over the mossy toys of childhood.
Embroidered stories spark paper witches in
wooden clogs clatter
and dance on druid gravestones
Wrapped in time and goblin magic
clinging to the edge of haunted
hallowed turf.
People of the land talk of the myth
an old lady far away

Chapter 8

I have a good memory for those days. She looked as if she had. Her eyes were the eyes of one who can remember; one whose childhood does not fade like a dream, nor whose youth vanish like a sunbeam. She would not take life, loosely and incoherently, in parts, and let one season slip as she entered on another: she would retain and add ... and so grow in harmony and consistency as she grew in years.[43]

Popping yer clogs, passing away, pushing up daisies and meeting yer Maker were just a few of the metaphors my mother used when forced to allude to death. Unlike her Brontë friends who wrote of death in its intensity, Rosalie was of a generation that could not talk about their own mortality. It is not as if you can blame them. Living through two world wars, her parents' generation experienced extreme fear, suffering, bereavement and death – and lived with the scars and trauma. As children of the Second World War, our Rosie's generation also had their share of distress and horror. For our little girl, death and suffering were a lived reality. Working-class life in the industrial north of England was marked by poverty, deprivation, loss and the fallout of the 1914–1918 war, which continued to play out in the memory of her parents and grandparents.

The idea that we carry the trauma and grief of our ancestors is not new. As family history flows through generations, the past lives and characteristics of those in our blood line patterns and repatterns shame, trauma and grief. I have two snapshot memories of my paternal grandfather. One is of him showing me a cuckoo clock that Uncle Tony had brought back from a holiday in Switzerland. Grandad loved making me laugh by moving the hands around and making the little wooden bird pop out of its tiny door above the clock face. The other memory of my grandad is not so pleasing, for across his back was a huge scar. Purple and puckered with age, it was his war wound. At the age of twenty, he had joined up with an East Lancashire 'pals' regiment and was wounded at the Battle of the Somme. Throughout his life, Grandad was known for 'doing a Heathcliff'. He was moody and violent, easily triggered to both outbursts of temper and long periods of silence. On reflection, one can only assume he lived with undiagnosed post-traumatic stress and was in pain throughout his life. Nevertheless, he was a difficult man who made the lives of his family traumatic in turn. Death came peacefully at the age of seventy when he fell asleep in his armchair by the fire and never woke up. Always one to bury the bad and to never speak ill of the dead, my mother often said, 'Thank God for small mercies. He suffered enough in life'. And with that, his behaviour became myth, leaving in its trail a long shadow of sorrow and forced acceptance.

In our Rosie's world, as in generations before her, birth and death took place in the home and community. As in the Brontë stories, womenfolk looked after their own, moving from sickbed to sickbed, offering comfort and ministering the duties that come with birth and dying. Midwives to the newborn and to the dead, they washed the corpses of family, friends and neighbours and laid them in the front parlour. The community came to pay their respects, and the menfolk dug the graves. Like all children, my mother was dragged along to view the bodies of young and old and witnessed the rituals that come with death. Most people could not afford to pay for a doctor, leaving many of them struggling too. At the age of six, my mother had an operation to remove an ovarian cyst. Her overriding memory of this time was of shame, as her parents could not afford the doctor's fee. The doctor's wife stood on the doorstep and asked, 'What is the use of an old vase when my children have holes in their shoes?' In the months that were to be the end of her life, my mother remembered the disgrace of that day and the guilt she carried for taking more than her fair share. On the back of an envelope, shoved into one of her diaries, she wrote, 'No NHS at the time. It took years to pay off the doctor's bill at sixpence a week'.

Then the NHS came along; Aneurin Bevan, God love him, had a vision of free health care for all from the 'cradle to the grave'. His welcomed promise, to take it all away, to give over life and death to trained professionals and hide it behind closed hospital doors. Shiny new babies and wholesome young mothers emerged into the sunlight, sterile, healthy and clean. At the other end – the grave I mean – well we won't talk about that. 'It is all taken care of these days,' my mother would say with blessed relief. Death is now washed away. Dead bodies now cared for by nurses, taken on trolleys to be stored in mortuaries until the vast amount of multicoloured paperwork, that comes with mortal demise, is completed. A van with darkened windows, driven by men in shiny black suits, now take away the dead – never to be seen again. This was progress and meant that my parents' generation could get on with thriving and rebuilding the country. And they did. But *it* didn't go away, so deeply was it buried in memory and psyche. As a result, fear and childhood traumas festered through decades of breathtaking transformation, through the millennium and beyond into a world scarred by the COVID-19 pandemic, climate emergency and more and more war.

The world changed so much for those 1930s war kids. As our Rosie would so often protest, 'Anything goes these days.' But the one taboo remaining is talking about death. And that is a problem. The children of the Second World War are now the older generation in their eighties and nineties. They may be able to talk about death in detached matter-of-fact terms but so often cannot talk about their own death and dying. What is more, they have bred children and grandchildren who can't talk about it either. Death and sex were the two unmentionable subjects in our house. When broached, my mother's tiny hand would shoot up as a signal that the conversation was not going any further. *'Ptt-ptt-ptt,'* she would cluck. 'I won't talk about t'graveyard till I have to stop there.'

In 2016, and for the second time, our Rosie was diagnosed with cancer. This particular chapter in her life had begun twenty-five years earlier at the age of sixty, when a tumour was found on her lung. I remember from that time, how she handled it in her typical, stoic, resilient way. We were under strict instructions that there were to be no hugs, tears or words of sympathy. Nor were we to talk about death. Her father had died of lung cancer at the age of sixty and now naturally, history was repeating itself. 'It is what it is,' she would say. It was a difficult time, as she seemed to harden, close in on herself and draw on some solitary, deeper strength. She was fearful, angry and bitter, blaming the cancer on her hard life, family and all that she had been 'put through' over the years.

As her daughter I felt pushed away, abandoned, racked with guilt and shamed for my part in her illness. There was a real, tangible fear and likelihood that my mother would die, but as her family, we respected her wishes, holding the love and continuing to show up as she underwent a huge operation that involved removing a lobe of her right lung. Even though I was a nurse, to see my mother so ill and my father so anxious was shocking and scary. At first, supporting her to wash and dress, slowly easing her tense body to relieve pain and find comfort, was awkward for both of us. Yet there was a gentle grace. In our shared vulnerability, our mother–daughter relationship began to mature. I came to see my mother as a woman beyond a parent. The tenderness and gratitude nurtured then grew over the years and came into its own when, at the age of forty-nine, I became a widow with two children to bring up alone.

Caring for my husband as he journeyed with cancer evoked a deep feeling of remembering. I had done this before. There were days when he was too ill for conversation, too weak and worn out to say thank you or I love you; but it did not mean that the love was not there. Like my mother, he sometimes only had the strength to go inwards, or simply just to carry on breathing or swallow a sip of water. Walking to the toilet left him exhausted and grumpy. As with my mother previously, there were times when he would snap and be cruel. Sometimes we are called to accept what is unacceptable, but I knew what I had to do. I had done it before and recognised that my job was to show up, to gently be alongside and always, always to hold kindness, compassion and dignity.

My husband died on a foggy November afternoon. At home, in bed, we knew the end was close. His cancer was so advanced, by the time he was diagnosed, he was beyond treatment. Weak and weary, emaciated and exhausted, he turned to me and said, 'I have had enough.' I stroked his arm and said, 'I know.' An hour later, he was dead. It happened so quickly in the end. He did not fade into unconsciousness as I imagined he would. He was resting and, worn out by days and nights without sleep, I dozed on the bed next to him. Suddenly, he sat up and swung his legs to get out of bed. This was not surprising, as he had been suffering with extreme diarrhoea and vomiting for several days. I rushed round the bed to help him. 'Oh, you are there,' were the last words he spoke as he fell into my arms. With his head on my shoulder, the last thing he saw were golden leaves, showering from the beech tree outside the bedroom window. Nine minutes later, he was gone.

Ancient vaccary walls, Wycoller

Chapter 9

Gentle reader, may you never feel what I then felt! May your eyes never shed such stormy, scalding, heart-wrung tears as poured from mine[44]

As the seasons fell into each other and winter rolled in, grey, damp, dark days were a mirror to my grief and bereavement. Christmas came and went in a fog of dense sadness and physical pain. My heart and chest ached with heaviness. My face throbbed with tension, and my mouth developed a strange twitch from forcing it to smile and to speak. I was dead inside, and the world carried on regardless. There is a Buddhist teaching that says: when the student is ready, the teacher will come. And so it was to unfold. One January afternoon, worn out and drained, I lit the log fire, took *Jane Eyre* off the shelf and curled up on the sofa beneath a blanket of Yorkshire wool. The crimp of parched paper and the creased lines of the tatty spine moulded her into my hands. My old friend, Jane Eyre. She had taught me so much about how to be a woman in a cruel world, how to stand up to bullies, to love and to forgive. Against all the odds she was rooted in and gave voice to her values and sense of self. My guide and counsellor, Jane Eyre became my companion in grief.

'Fiction must stick to facts, and the truer the facts, the better the fiction' wrote Virginia Woolf.[45] Being with dying brings in its wake vivid memories and raw emotion that, even when buried for years can explode to the surface unexpectedly. A smell, a taste, a glance, a touch, a sound of birdsong, poetry or music may all spark the embers of visceral grief. A review of *Jane Eyre*, written in 1847 suggested 'it *is* an autobiography, not, perhaps, in the naked facts and circumstances, but in the actual suffering and experience'.[46] Then as now, one cannot read *Jane Eyre* through a lens of grief without connecting to the life of Charlotte Brontë and her siblings. Following the death of their mother, an eyewitness to the goings-on in Haworth Parsonage said of the children, 'they were grave and silent beyond their years … you would not have known there was a child in the house, they were such still, noiseless, good little creatures'.[47] Little Jane Eyre, lonely, motherless and frightened, wrapped herself in scarlet curtain drapes to hide from the outside world.

Witnessing the raw grief of my own children, the image is one of a womb-like space, where a small child just wants to feel safe again. My children too would often crawl into a space and curl into a foetal ball. Head down, knees drawn and arms covering their sad faces, their beds and duvets became a blank space where I could not reach them except with broken-hearted love. Jane Eyre, the bereaved child, unloved and abandoned, became the outsider. Separated from the world, she was a forsaken little soul who observed the living, through an invisible veil. *Jane Eyre*, created by Charlotte Brontë, gave voice to a grieving young girl, who continued to reach out across generations with honesty, truth and hope. The death of a loved one ushers in a new life that is never, ever the same, as loss is integrated and folded into the everyday. As the bereaved move from loving in presence to loving in absence,[48] the experience becomes a part of who you are, shaping how you see the world and inviting healing through creativity and time.

Virginia Woolf also alluded to the healing and therapeutic quality of writing as a way of connecting and reordering past events and making sense of grief and trauma. Charlotte Brontë was five years old when her mother died. Brother Branwell was four, Emily three and baby Anne twenty months old. By the time she was eight, Charlotte's elder sisters Maria and Elizabeth had also died.[49] So much tragedy, pain, loss and abandonment for those tiny children to bear. It is no wonder that they escaped to the moors and created the imaginary worlds of Angria and Gondal, where they had control and the power to bring the dead back to life. That is what death does to us. For a while, it draws us into a space that is not quite living, and yet ironically, life goes on. In time, we may slowly go back into the land of the living but never with the same eye. It is not surprising that as an adult, Charlotte wrote to a friend that she had started to study people from about the age of five.[50] Arguably, she carried this skilled, deep analysis of humanity with her throughout life, her personal experience of childhood bereavement becoming part of who she was and an energy that fed her genius and creativity. When young Jane Eyre, the orphaned outsider, is punished by her cruel Aunt Reed by being incarcerated overnight in a spooky red room, one cannot help but ponder if Charlotte was drawing on childhood experience when she wrote of 'such dread as children only can feel'.[51] How do children speak of what they see? 'Children can feel, but they cannot analyse their feelings; and if the analysis is partially effected in thought, they know not how to express the result of the process in words'.[52] And who would listen anyway?

Back to the sofa and the Yorkshire wool blanket; I see for the first time Brontë's stroke of genius, as the reader is invited to witness death through a child's eyes. In an almost Alice in Wonderland moment, I shrink to a ten-year-old self and stand alongside Jane Eyre as 'a light shone through the keyhole, and from under the door; a profound stillness pervaded the vicinity'. I walk with her as she enters the room and moves towards the bedside. 'My hand was on the curtain, but I preferred speaking before I withdrew it. I still recoiled at the dread of seeing a corpse. "Helen"! I whispered softly; "are you awake?".'[53] It is well acknowledged that the death of Helen Burns is based on Charlotte's elder sister Maria, but it is not unreasonable to imagine this may also be a memory of a marginalised child witnessing her mother's death. And so, my broken heart breaks even more. I weep buckets of tears as little Jane Eyre climbs onto the bed, clings on to, and protects her dying friend Helen Burns. 'I got on to her crib and kissed her: her forehead was cold, and her cheek both cold and thin, and so were her hand and wrist: but she smiled as of old'.[54] I do not need to imagine what it is like to be alongside when children witness the death of a loved one. I have been there and tasted the bewilderment and fear, as their fledgling arms reach out to warm the shivering body of the one, who in a normal world, would be their protector.

If *Jane Eyre* is anything, it is a book about childhood bereavement, raw humanity, rage and courage. 'Here I lay again crushed and trodden on',[55] Brontë writes. Throwing down the gauntlet, our heroine Jane Eyre challenges the status quo and tackles the existential questions of the bereaved, such as who and where is God. No doubt a risky business in 1847, especially for the daughter of a churchman. And yet *Jane Eyre* always leads the reader through turmoil towards renewed hope, peace and healing in nature. 'Is it all over? Have you cried your grief away?'.[56] Walking in the garden of her impoverished school, little Jane ponders, 'a greenness grew over those brown beds, which, freshening daily, suggested the thought that Hope traversed them at night, and left each morning brighter traces of her steps'.[57] And so, to heal my broken heart, I fell unexpectedly into a Brontë marathon, seeing with fresh eyes how much they knew of grief. Reading again the books, poetry and letters of Charlotte, Emily and Anne, I came to find out more about how their lives were shaped by loss, how the light of security and home had refracted and narrowed to become a dark tunnel of abandonment and how eventual hope brought green shoots of recovery. I pondered if I had the right to bring a 21st-century perspective to the Brontë story but I could not help it. With two bereaved children of my own, our little world devastated by grief, I needed help and the evidence was overwhelming.

Brontë Parsonage

Chapter 10

I see a white cheek and a faded eye, but no trace of tears. I suppose, then, your heart has been weeping blood[58]

On a steep learning curve, I came to understand the complexity of my new life. Like Patrick Brontë, I unexpectedly found myself a single parent and was desperate to find out as much as I could to support my children and rebuild stability and security from the rubble of our shattered lives. And there it was in front of me, the lives and works of the Brontës, played out patterns of grief and bereavement that were mirrored in my own being and life experience. Emulating a 21st-century approach and understanding of loss, they emerged, signposting me out of the mess.

It is easy to airbrush the early childhood experiences of the Brontës out of history. As in all the towns of the 19th-century industrial north, poverty was rife and disease rampant. Exploitation, child labour, overcrowded housing and a lack of clean water and sanitation meant that life was grim – and death was cruel. Haworth Parsonage, the home of the Brontë children, is still framed by a packed graveyard. Moss-covered, tilted headstones crowd the space between the house and church. Faded names repeat themselves across generations. Babies and children, mothers, sisters, husbands and sons, many of whom died within weeks of each other, are a pitiless reminder of the sweeping randomness of hunger, malnutrition, consumption and cholera. Such ugly and appalling scenarios may have been the norm, but it does not mean that in that pool of raw, shared humanity, the pain and impact was any less than it is today.

The death of a parent or sibling is the worst kind of childhood loss. The poor Brontë children had a triple whammy. Within the space of four years, their mother died, probably of uterine cancer, followed by the tragic loss of two elder sisters, Maria aged eleven and Elizabeth aged ten. All died in the family home, and all were buried in the church, yards from their garden gate. One can only wonder what these children saw and imagine their bewilderment. What went through their young minds? How did it feel? How did they make sense of unfolding events? Every day of their lives, from their bedroom windows, they saw the church where their mother and sisters lay under stone flags. On Sundays, perhaps they walked over their bodies – so close and yet so far. Day in, day out, graves were dug, and their father conducted funeral after funeral at their own front door. A grisly image indeed, one that is deeply disturbing, almost gothic in the 21st century. Times may change but feelings stay the same. As bereaved children today are encouraged to play and act out their understanding, the Brontë children created a safe place in their heads. In games and stories, they could be together and let their imaginations and creativity run wild.

As my husband became increasingly ill, the energy in our home became subdued and heavy. What had been a hub of activity and raucous play transformed into silent space, hidden behind a veil of sadness and pale childlike masks of solemnity. Elizabeth Gaskell's portrayal of motherless children, living isolated lives on the edge of a desolate Yorkshire moor, has become a cornerstone of the Brontë legend. Interviewing first-hand witnesses from that time, Gaskell wrote that Maria was too ill to take care of, or even see, her children and Patrick was too busy. Aloof and alone, 'the six little creatures used to walk out, hand in hand, towards the glorious wild moors, which in after days they loved so passionately; the elder ones taking thoughtful care of the toddling wee things'.[59] Behind the house, the children stepped out onto the moors into a world beyond the graveyard. With freedom to roam and play, they delved into imaginary worlds, where goblins and fairy folk dwell and where they had the power to bring the dead back to life, just by wishing it. Weaving local myth and legend into a fantasy world, these insular, bereaved children had control over their lives. And so, we come to the early collective writing of the Brontë siblings. Known as the juvenilia, the tales of Glass Town, Angria and Gondal began in childhood bereavement and laid the foundation for their future dreams of becoming authors.

In the 21st century, the experience and long-term impact of childhood bereavement is better understood. For example, it is appreciated that one way of coping with bereavement is to escape into one's own head and that withdrawal is a normal response to grief and trauma.[60] In creating their imaginary world, the Brontë children found a safe place, where resilience, love, tragedy and pain could be on their terms and where their anxieties and questions could be aired. Trying to make sense of actual events and the words adults use is confusing. What is cancer? What is consumption? Can I catch it? Did I do something to make it happen? Is it my fault? What will happen to the body? What about me? These are questions young children carry but so often grown-ups do not have the language or the courage to explain. It is not unusual for children to be fearful of catching the disease that has proved fatal to their loved one. So vivid is the memory of my own son, aged ten, asking me if he could catch his daddy's cancer and if he was going to die. In one of the stories of Glass Town, our young authors pronounce, 'when the grave closed on Marian, a nervous dread took possession of his mind lest the seeds of the mother's malady might have been transmitted to the child'.[61]

They refer to funerals, vaults, rattling bones, the 'ineradicable upas-tree of consumption'[62] and of one who was only eight weeks in dying. In the matter-of-fact way of children, they go on to describe the cruel pattern of the disease:

> He seems to have no more than perhaps a week's strength in him, that is to say, my girl, when respiration begins to rattle in his throat and the infernal brightness dies off his cheek and his flesh (the little that remains) grows perfectly transparent, showing no blood but bones.[63]

As a nurse, I have witnessed what they described in their stories. The rattling sound of an altered breathing pattern and waxy, pallid skin are signs of a body in transition to death. From reading the fantasies of the Brontë children, I came to learn so much. Who could have known that their games and stories, acted out in childhood could offer a guide to a bereaved and befuddled me?

Death is the worst kind of abandonment. When a parent dies, the rug is pulled – as the one person who is supposed to protect, care and love unconditionally is no longer there. It is not surprising then that an adult who has been bereaved as a child may well have difficulty trusting others, as the fear of being abandoned again simmers and spills over into other relationships. I have come to know that in the 21st century there is an increasing understanding and appreciation of the impact of childhood bereavement, although it often gets overlooked when anger kicks in. Evidence suggests that trauma from the death of a significant other may have a devastating long-term impact on adults bereaved as children, if grief is unresolved.[64] The Brontës were bereaved children, who as adults were hidden mourners, as they continued to grieve and pine for their mother and sisters. The ghosts that haunted their lives created characters who were abandoned, orphaned, frustrated, angry and disturbed, all striving in their own way to find love and a place of belonging. Cut through the monster that is Heathcliff and what do you see? An abandoned child, so blinded by anger, driven by an overwhelming sense of injustice, who cannot see beyond his own twisted pain. Storming around *Wuthering Heights*, threatening to crush those in his path 'like a sparrow's egg',[65] ultimately knowing that he is the one crushed. What today we would call complicated grief, Heathcliff is the extreme representation of a broken anguished child in an adult body. So damaged by cruel loss and abuse, he went to extreme, dark depths of human behaviour to be loved.

The genius of Charlotte, Emily and Anne, their unique grasp of human experience, love and loss still reaches out a hand across the centuries to touch soul and spirit of the dear reader today. With my own experience of loss, I have come to judge less and understand more. Everyone I see, in every situation, I now ask myself: what is their story? For Branwell Brontë, the churning childhood emotions of abandonment, guilt and shame became an increasingly complex, downward spiral of low self-esteem and self-worth, and it seems that he was alone in struggling with his personal demons. His fall into addiction took a huge emotional toll on the wider family. Pulling no punches, in her direct, no-nonsense way, Charlotte wrote to a friend, 'I wish I could say one word to you in his favour – but I cannot – therefore I will hold my tongue'.[66] In other words, as my mother would so often caution, 'If you can't say owt nice, say nowt.'

For 200 years, Branwell has been judged for his failings and bad behaviour. Without detracting from his adult responsibility, it may be worth sparing a moment to consider if the adult Branwell was at the same time a bereaved child, numbing out the pain with risk-taking behaviour and inappropriate relationships. A sad picture of emerging 21st-century studies suggests that little has changed. Left unsupported in the complexity of grief, adults bereaved as children are at a higher risk of experiencing mental health problems including depression, anxiety and substance misuse.[67, 68] The experiences of my mother, grandmothers and great-grandmothers have shown how difficult it can be to live with toxic, bullying and abusive behaviour. There are no excuses of course, but there are reasons. I ponder now, what was the root of the pain, for my ancestors, for Branwell and Heathcliff? What is the story behind what we see?

Re-establishing continuity and routine in a bereaved family is of huge importance, and the involvement of a significant, stable other adult is desirable, not least to support the grieving parent left behind. For the Brontë children and for Patrick, this came in the form of the maternal Aunt Branwell. With a gaping hole in their lives, the family adjusted to loss. Home became a creative place where, in their 'other' world of imagination, they were safe and secure together. As life went on at the Parsonage, their mother and sisters lay under stone flags in the family vault a few yards away. Maybe I am thinking too deeply to suggest that the choice of name, Glass Town, was pointed. Was home, the moor and the imaginary world they created a mirror into another world? Or perhaps it was in this place of play and fantasy that these children peered through a looking glass of grief, to observe a devastated and distant living parent and a new everyday reality.

Life does indeed go on. As with the Brontë children, I began to see it through an opaque lens of detachment, death and survival. Blown apart by cancer, adjusting to a different life was complicated, as days, weeks and months ticked by without my husband. A widowed, single mum, I found myself 300 miles away from my own increasingly frail and ailing mother, herself a cancer survivor.

Being with her whilst at the same time trying to support and steer my children through months and years without their dad was difficult – almost impossible in fact. And yet there were moments of grace and magic. Crushing grief and my mother's failing health somehow came together in a place of mother–daughter comfort. My devastation penetrated her forgetfulness and found a place in memory. She sensed my pain and in silence, her arms opened to gather me up as she had always done. 'Keep putting one foot in front of another love. Remember where you came from' were her only words of wisdom. Strangely, at the most harrowing and challenging of times, I was strengthened by my roots and able to draw on the resilience of the women who had gone before me. My grandmothers and great-grandmothers had lived through hard times too and had done it with courage, humour, grit and each other. Restored, comforted and with fresh insight and understanding, the time came to return *Jane Eyre* and *Wuthering Heights* to the shelf. Time to fold up the woollen blanket, to dust myself down and, in the spirit of Charlotte Brontë, take 'the only radical cure for rooted sorrow'[69] and get on with it.

Chapter 11

Reading is my favourite occupation, when I have leisure for it, and books to read[70]

Sadly, my husband's journey with cancer was short. Three months from the day of diagnosis, he died in my arms. In contrast, and against all the odds, our Rosalie pulled through her first encounter with the nasty disease. Weakened and never quite the same, she nevertheless 'lived to tell the tale', as she so often said. And tell the tale she certainly did. She even lived long enough to cough up the stitches from her lung. The doctor was baffled and speechless, but the evidence was there. After twenty years, three black stitches, like squashed spiders, were wrapped up in toilet paper and hidden for safekeeping behind the marble clock on the mantelpiece. And that, dear reader, was my mother all over. The feisty little woman who survived lung cancer against the odds.

The intervening twenty-five years between the first cancer and its inevitable reoccurrence were what our Rosie called a blessing. She believed that God, for some reason, had spared her and marvelled, as over the years she held in her arms four more grandchildren and a great-grandson. 'God is good', she would say. We became a family who had been touched irrevocably by cancer. Life changed forever as I moulded visits and holidays around my mother's health. I learned to be flexible, to go with the ebb and flow of her pattern of illness. Cherishing his precious one, my father wrapped her in cotton wool, fiercely protecting her from the outside world and anything that might compromise her fragile health. Woe betide anyone who came within a mile of her with the slightest sniffle. On the one hand, it was frustrating to see her world shrink, but with maturity and reflection, I see that this was her choice and her right. She determined to live her remaining years with intention and love, surrounding herself with what mattered – family and books.

A self-taught autodidact, my mother was a highly intelligent woman who, through a love of books and reading, held a wealth of knowledge about most things. For over fifty years, she was my first and constant teacher and my 'go-to' person whenever I had something exciting to share. My mother could recall facts at the click of a finger, often astounding herself and those around her with the breadth of her wisdom. Even in her later years, her sharpened mind would mean that she could answer any question on history, geography, politics or literature. Though she could barely see, when read aloud, crosswords and sudoku were a doddle. So scarred was she by deprivation, poverty and duty, she undermined her own intelligence, worth and gifts by saying, 'but I only know rubbish.' An absence of education and quashed girlhood dreams of being a teacher left our Rosie without confidence in her ability, forever believing that her head was 'only full of nonsense' and what she knew was worthless trivia.

As a working-class child of the 1930s and 40s, the deprivation was not merely financial. Unlike the Brontë sisters, whose education and learning were nurtured by their clerical father, little Rosie had no such support. The school and community reinforced the status quo, that a girl's ambition must be to become a good wife and mother. In later years, as stories of the past became more and more prolific, it became apparent that the lack of encouragement and opportunity for her education was a deep source of regret and a sadness that my mother carried throughout her life. The misogynistic power of the parish priest forbade poor girls like my mother from taking entrance exams for the grammar school believing this would detract from their God-given purpose in life. Always recalling fondly her dear dad, when she came to talk about her mother, memories were of the harsh but necessary choices she made. When Rosie won a scholarship to attend a secretarial school at the age of fourteen, her mother pulled her out after a few weeks and sent her to work in the cotton mill as a six-loom weaver. 'You see, the family needed the five pounds a week I could earn there', she explained. As ever, our Rosie chose to count her blessings and would always speak of her love and gratitude for a wonderful marriage and family. And yet, as frailty and vulnerability crept in, the shadow side emerged. Shrugging in surrender to the choices that had never been hers, she accepted, 'We couldn't afford it. That is how it was.' Her continued sense of loyalty and duty, that her role at the age of fourteen was to do her bit to support the family, was accepted without question.

The years in the mill were recollected in detail, often manifesting in disturbing dreams. The 5 am wake-up call, six days a week, and the two-mile walk for a 6.30 am start were the fun parts of the day. Along the way, our Rosie was joined by family, neighbours and friends, all heading in the same direction for a hard day's work. 'We all wore clogs. Mine were brown with a brass buckle', she wrote. 'In all weathers we would hold hands and slither down the hill'. Well used clogs needed regular repair. 'At the cloggers we all just sat on a bench in our stocking feet waiting for our irons or rubbers to be done'. On occasions I witnessed my mother's eyes and mind wandering for a few seconds before coming back with a jolt. She would vehemently shake her head, scrunch up her eyes, lift and wave her hand to holt the flow of unwelcome memories. My mother had hated working in the mill. It was noisy, dirty, exhausting, soul-destroying and there were enormous spiders. The outside toilets were across the mill yard and a girl's pay would be docked should she be caught short outside of the dinner break. Some of the overlookers, or 'tatlers' as they were known, were kind, but most were nasty bullies. 'And to have that as your place of work at fourteen was horrid,' she said. There were things my mother did not want to remember, confidences that must be kept and secrets she would take to the grave. Our lovely Rosie's life had been hard, the legacy of which was a tough little woman with a steely determination that life would be better for her own children. Her daughters would be educated, have the opportunities denied to her and never, ever be forced to work in a mill.

Mine was an education that was lived on the cusp of the secondary modern and comprehensive educational transition of the late 1960s and early 70s. On reflection, it was basic and of a poor standard and, like my mother's, echoed the aspirations of the class system. It was a time when opportunity for working-class girls was becoming possible – though not really expected. Career options on offer generally fell into the categories of nursing or teaching. Having been robbed of the chance of education themselves, my parents were determined that their bright girl would make the most of what was on offer. They heartily and determinedly encouraged, nay, pushed me to pursue education and life away from my hometown. It brought adventure, travel and a blessed career in nursing. When I met my husband-to-be, our second date was to Haworth, where we shared a cream tea for my birthday treat. After all, I had to check him out on the Brontë barometer. I was both startled and relieved that he didn't feature on the scale. A quiet, deep, hard-working, intelligent and steady man, he was an unfamiliar character and thus fascinating to me. He passed the test of course, but the connection to landscape, my native home, was something he never understood.

My mother was nothing if not a woman of contradiction. Although she accepted my choice, she never understood my husband's strange, southern ways of having lunch at dinnertime and dinner at teatime – or his insistence of having a cup of tea or coffee rather than a brew. Forever known as 'yon feller', my darling husband was never really accepted for who he was; nor was he wholly forgiven for taking me away. With a sense of belonging that defined her, she was proud of her ancestry and Irish Lancastrian roots and never wished to be anywhere else. She would often say to me, 'Nell, you have been homesick all your life.' And yet when I spoke of a longing to return home, I was always met with a northern bluntness, 'What do you want to do that for? There is nothing for you here.' She always believed that somehow, for me, life elsewhere was better. But she was wrong. For what was there was family, the landscape, the view from the window, my roots. That was home.

My children have had a different life. They never knew a school holiday when they weren't bundled into the car and driven across the country to Lancashire. Endless half-term holidays have passed, walking to Wycoller, paddling in the freezing beck and snacking on crisps and chocolate in the fireplace ruin of Ferndean Manor. Frequent visits to warm cafés and pubs in and around Haworth were treats and compensation for being dragged around the Parsonage Museum. As ever, at the end of chilly northern days, we sat around the fire, in the shadow of the gold-embossed frame of *Wuthering Heights*. In conversation with Grandma Rosie, they too became fluent in family history. Each visit, as regular as clockwork, my father would roll his eyes, as from the sideboard cupboard my mother pulled a timeworn shoe box. The blue striped pattern and imprint of a stiletto heel yielded a tale of a pair of high heel black patent leather shoes bought in the 1960s for 'some fancy do or another'. The shoes were long gone but the box lived on, to host an archive of family photographs. On lifting the lid, curls of black and white pictures of all shapes and sizes spewed out onto the fireside rug. In my mother's experience, photographs were a rarity, commanding everyone to show up in their Sunday best for weddings, day trips to Blackpool and bus rides to Haworth. A handful of snapshots revealed more casual poses, such as Granny Vi doing a cartwheel on Blackpool sands and a teenage Rosalie alongside an elephant in Phoenix Park Dublin in 1949. Another photograph was of my parents on the day they were engaged. Arms around each other's waists, heads tilted back in laughter, my mother's curly hair was loose and blowing in the wind. Even in the depths of her forgetfulness and frailty, our Rosie held on to the memory of that day, bringing colour and life to the black and white image, as she described in detail the folds of her woollen skirt, the bow on her blue shoes and the white leather handbag my father had bought her. Such were the ramblings of an old lady, and all is history now. Consequently, for my children, family are distant folk. Theirs is a different sense of belonging and I can't help feeling that somewhere on the M6 motorway, on the long road between North and South, something was lost along the way.

The ruins of Wycoller Hall

Chapter 12

I was grieved for the overthrow of all our air-built castles[71]

Following her first encounter with cancer, my mother's health was never the same. I am sad and regret missed opportunities to take her on outings to her beloved Haworth, to share her memories of places unchanged and her joy in the new. Mum loved to hear stories of the Parsonage Museum and new exhibitions of Brontë treasures. Her eyes lit up when I spoke of shops full of books, populated by visitors from across the globe and quaint cafés full of scones and chocolate cake. With fondness and deep affection, she remembered the steep cobbled streets of the town, walks along the edge of Haworth to Penistone Craggs, the Brontë Falls and beyond, to Top Withins, where the breathtaking views of endless miles of moorland and heather pointed towards home. Decades passed and, in truth, our Rosie didn't go out for years. Never quite up to it, she always made excuses that she was too tired, that the weather was too cold, wet, or perhaps there was snow on the way. As cancer and subsequent frailty emerged simultaneously, our wise matriarch took up residence by the fire. Despite failing eyesight, she pored over world events. From her threadbare rocking chair, the brown floral, printed pattern, faded with age and sunlight, she scrutinised family goings-on with equal relish. With a sense and reality of place, the story never changed, and even on her dying day, she looked out on the moor and the mythical space towards the Heights.

As health and memory began to deteriorate, my mother began to have a real sense of urgency to tell her story. 'Write this down; you need to know,' she would say. 'Write a book, our Nell.' On her 86th birthday, she was given a notebook, and for two years, up to her last weeks, our Rosie avidly charted cherished memories of childhood and family, the sad repetition, reflecting her increasing memory loss. Her writing spilled out to the front and back covers, bits of paper, used napkins and even a chocolate box lid sufficed in her urgency to write. There was no order or chronology to it; the words just poured out, endless lists of long-gone uncles, aunts, cousins and friends, who married who, who did what and when. On the back of photographs and in the margins of photograph albums, she recorded hatches and dispatches, the dates of births, deaths and marriages of loved ones. Over the years, my mother had an increasing preoccupation of checking the local paper for obituaries. As time went on, this weekly ritual shifted from being one of empathic interest to a sad reality. My mother was almost the last of her generation. Stoic and resigned to loss, she found comfort in faith but was increasingly lonely, missing friends she had shared her life with. When my father's obituary appeared, she circled it in pen and wrote alongside, 'I did it MY WAY. He made a good job of his life'.

It may seem strange to say that in the days following my father's death her diary records nothing of his passing. On the night he died, her mind took her to a place where she remembered them together as children. Perhaps the reality and the pain were just too hard to bear. The next morning, on the back of her favourite photograph, dated 12 May 1939, the names of all the children in the picture were scrawled in a faint, wobbly hand. She wrote how one girl, her best friend, had later died of scarlet fever and another of consumption. And in the margin scrawled, 'No treatment. No NHS. The NHS is great!' Side by side in this formal school picture were my parents, Frank (age seven) and Rosalie O'Riley (age eight), both dressed in their Sunday best. My mother cherished the connection they shared as family, friends and neighbours. She could not remember a time when they did not live and work together, sharing the joys and sorrows of life. In one of her diary entries, my mother wrote 'one day Frank and his brothers stayed most of the day at our house while their mam was giving birth to a baby girl. Sadly, not to be'. My grandmothers could not have been closer than when alongside each other in childbirth and loss. I wonder how they felt when they stood together watching their children marry or held the grandchildren they shared. There is something strangely comforting in the knowledge that my grandparents and great-grandparents were so close and were alongside each other through thick and thin. My grandfathers died within six weeks of each other, and it was always believed that the one left behind died of a broken heart. Unlike my life, lived away from kinfolk, my mother never had to fill in gaps or explain who was who. In her world, she knew everyone – and they knew her. That was a safe place to be.

Alongside the sadness and joy of memories, my mother constantly made notes and shopping lists. In what was to become a four-volume diary epic, she chronicled the minutiae of everyday life in an attempt to hang on to her slipping, short-term memory and hold back the tide of forgetfulness. All visitors, be they family, friends, doctors, or carers, were invited to do the same. In quiet moments and in long hours of sleepless nights, it is evident that my mother read these contributions. Her sharp wit shows her correcting facts, punctuation and spelling in the same way she always had. Regular inventories of what she had for tea, weather updates and her continued obsession with being warm enough, remained testimony to the woman I had always known. As in life, her writing was full of gratitude. She never grumbled or asked, 'why me?', rather she continued to count her blessings as she had always done. Listing family, friends, children and even past pets, she would write, 'Thank God for them. I am blessed. Wonderful family. More blessings than we ever dreamed of. I feel very happy'. When frailty took over and my mother took to her bed, her gratitude was endless. 'Lovely chocolate. Thank you to whoever brought it'. 'I am enjoying my bowl of porridge and thinking of other people and times less fortunate'. 'God bless and thanks for my beautiful warm blanket. God bless all the knitters. Keep the needles going! My favourite pastime once. Five children = lots of jumpers!' At the end of her life, our Rosie became the lady with the notebook, a storyteller, a wisewoman. That is who she was and who she will always remain in my heart and memory.

One of the greatest inventions in my mother's latter years was the iPad. There she would sit, holding court, as we shared a cup of tea together across the miles. She never ceased to be amazed by such a miracle. There were lots of laughs as grandchildren shared with her the wonders of YouTube. She was thrilled to see her old favourites, such as Frank Sinatra and Glenn Miller and would sing along to songs and musicals, laughing as she remembered her dad's assertion that it wasn't proper music and would never last. 'I am enjoying remembering', my mother often wrote and was off again, reminiscing about Saturday night trains to Blackpool and dances at the Tower Ballroom. She talked of how every Sunday evening after church she would meet girl friends to dance and sing along to records played on a wind-up gramophone. Going even further back, she recalled music from her early years and Irish roots, the songs of opera and of the old Music Halls that her parents loved:

> I remember my dad rocking me and singing 'When Irish Eyes are Smiling'. We had an old wind-up pink horn gramophone. 'Down at the Old Bull and Bush' my dad dancing with me in his arms. He was on the dole for 5 years. We did a lot of singing and dancing when we lived in the Circus Yard. My mother's favourite song was 'You are my Heart's Delight'.

My mother's first trip to London was as a woman in her 40s, when she went with my dad to see Sinatra, Liza Minnelli and Sammy Davis Jr at the Royal Albert Hall. Those were such happy intervals, but as time passed and the love of her life died, the diary records how memories of music became bittersweet, bringing joy and heartfelt tears in equal measure. In one such entry, she wrote, 'I thought Frank wakened me by tickling my feet and singing "Babyface" to make me laugh. I was always grumpy in the mornings. I have been dreaming again. I miss the sound of his voice'.

As memory loss increased, the iPad became something that my mother did not recognise. Similarly, she was not able to identify a mobile phone as a telephone. It was as if such modern contraptions were too recent to be embedded in memory; and so, both would ring and ring, becoming distant sounds that had nothing to do with her. Not unusually for those on a path of dementia, at times she experienced visual disturbances. A coat in the corner of the room became our old black Labrador dog and a handbag perched on the windowsill, a beautiful bowl of flowers. But alongside memory loss and frailty, there were periods when my mother would perk up. There were stints when her mind was sharp, recalling facts and figures instantly and solving crossword and sudoku puzzles, but increasingly, these moments became shorter and left her exhausted.

Chapter 13

How clear she shines! How quietly
I lie beneath her guardian light;
While heaven and earth are whispering me,
'Tomorrow, wake, but, dream tonight'.
Yes, Fancy, come, my Fairy love!
These throbbing temples softly kiss;
And bend my lonely couch above
And bring me rest, and bring me bliss[72]

Days turned into weeks, and weeks into months. My mother's advancing memory loss and care needs triggered intervention from health and social care services. An impersonal, mechanical hospital bed replaced the tattered old bed she had shared with my father, a sobering reminder of the reality of cancer, extreme fragility and increasing forgetfulness. As frailty progressed and independence diminished, the bed, chair and bathroom marked the corners of an invisible triangle in a shrinking world. With the aid of a walking frame with little wheels, our Rosie shuffled her tiny self to and from the bathroom. My mother had always loved clothes and enjoyed nothing more than shopping with her daughters. She never lost that interest and would regularly instruct me to open the wardrobe so that we could admire her clothes, coordinate outfits and chat about what she might like to wear the next day. But, in reality, in those latter years, she was often too weary to dress and would spend her days in her nightie with pretty, matching cardigans and little fluffy bed socks on her elfin feet. Walking behind to steady her wobbly gait as she pottered from bathroom to bed, I remember admiring her outfit, a beaded lilac cardigan over a pink nightie. 'You look bonny in that, Mum,' I said. Perching on the edge of the bed, she patted the space next to her, beckoning me to sit. As I did so, her hand reached out to stroke my face. 'My bonny girl,' she said as she nestled into my chest. I held her close, rocking her in my arms, softly kissing and stroking her white hair. Sometimes, she would notice a necklace or the rings on my hands and would twirl them gently in tender admiration. Such were the special mother–daughter moments and the touch that I miss so much.

Like most women of her age, my mother religiously visited the hairdressers every week for a shampoo and set. As cancer and frailty progressed, the precious ritual left her jaded, and as time wore on, even the visiting hairdresser was too much. Although the routine faded out of memory, with every trip to the bathroom, she would look in the mirror and 'tut' at the sight of thinning white, wild hair. 'I look like a witch,' she said, setting the intention to get her hair done the following week. It never happened. Instead, I would sit alongside and gently comb the soft feather of curls around my fingers. After a short time, she was exhausted by conversation and the three-metre hike to and from the toilet. Helping her to take off her slippers, I guided her little flake-skin legs back into bed, fluffed up her pillows, and in the twinkling of an eye, she dozed back into the land of nod.

Have no fear dear reader, for in her waking hours, my mother's stories continued unabated. When there was no one there to listen, she wrote of 'weaver girls in their flowers and ribbons'[73] and the fun and adventures they shared.

In 1945 a group of us girls went over to Dublin. When the war ended, we sailed across the sea to Ireland. We rode on an elephant called Sara in Phoenix Park and danced every night at the Crystal Ballroom. I bought a pair of white shoes and a box of food for five pounds because everything was still rationed at home.

Remembering her first date with Frank, she wrote,

I was wearing a navy-blue dress. The laugh with our group was 'don't ask to take Rosie home. Her mother is always waiting on the doorstep'. We had the last laugh when I married the boy from across the road. When he proposed to me on Morecambe Bay he said, 'you will marry me won't you' and I said, 'of course I will'. Real life isn't like the films you know. But my wedding dress was more beautiful than I could have expected, and I wore my white shoes as 'something old' on my wedding day, 6th June 1953. Coronation year.

It is not surprising that in the last two years of my mother's life, her once pristine handwriting became shaky, spindly and sometimes illegible. On further analysis, the diaries reveal how the deterioration in pen control mirrored long periods of pain, distress and confusion. Pain required medication, giving rise to a cycle of disorientation and angst as well as much-needed comfort and rest. Charting her pain, diary entries read, 'new day. Same Pain. Big ache. A poorly day'. Such writings were not unusual, and it became increasingly the norm that she would record her pain by listing the time:

1.15am
2.45
3am PAIN
3.45am Pain 4.45am Pain
5.30am 6am PAIN!!!!!

And then she would sleep peacefully for hours or slip into days and nights of more drug-induced disorientation and confusion. During these periods, three themes dominated her diaries: her early childhood experiences of poverty, the war and trying to make sense of disturbing dreams.

> BIG CHRISTMAS party given by the local Doctors. Presents. Mine was a pretty tea-party set. Never played with. Sold for £5 one Christmas when my dad was on the dole. It saw us thru. Was the Dole 32/6?

The first time little Rosalie saw a five pound note was as a school girl, when her teacher Miss Gibbs showed the class her salary. 'We thought she was so rich'. Recalling her preschool years, she went on to write,

> I remember watching my dad play billiards at Weavers Union before I started going to school. Mam played pop at him for having a tanner round double when he had no work and for buying me a small bag of tata crisps. My dad was on the dole for five years before the war. It was a sin and a shame on this country that intelligent men were out of work. There was plenty of work when the war came. He was too old for armed service and was sent to work on munitions for the army.

Another diary entry went on to explain how, one Christmas time, the local greengrocer gave her dad a dead rabbit, saying:

> 'I know it's not thy fault tha's out o' work lad'. My dad had spoken up as the weavers were not being paid the agreed union rate. When he spoke up he was sacked. Nobody backed him up. Everybody was too afraid (best say nowt!).

In the long nights, in the space between sleep and dreams, memories of the war brought back unwelcome experiences. Poverty rumbled on and rationing became the norm. My mother's diary recalls:

> We were playing out and Mrs Hartley passed by and said, 'War has been declared'. We didn't know what she meant. I was eight years old. Children from cities were evacuated away from the bombing. We took a little girl named Margaret and two boys from Manchester which was heavily bombed. One night Mam didn't come home. We were very worried as she was in Manchester and there was an air-raid. She got home the next day after spending the night in an air-raid shelter. The trains were cancelled as the steam trains could be seem by the enemy. The night sky would light up with bombs over Manchester but only one bomb dropped on our town.

My mother wrote repeatedly of this event, as it had been close to the houses where two aunts lived. 'I ran up next morning with mam to see the damage, but no one was killed'. A further story related a tale of my grandmothers:

> I remember my mother coming home from the shop saying she had just been talking to Edie and she saying how many months it was since she had heard from their Ronnie aged seventeen. He was serving in the navy. Pacific Ocean as it turned out.

As it also turned out, young Ronnie was my dad's big brother and my Uncle Ron. Another testimony to the web of loving, caring, maternal connection between my grandmothers.

Everyone was touched by war. Some survived and lived with the scars, but sadly, for many this was not the case. In another night-time narrative nightmare, our Rosie is 'wakened by a very sad dream, remembering heavy snow. The sledge run began in front of our house, a boy, an evacuee from Manchester, missed the runoff and went under a bus and died'. On another occasion, she wrote:

> I have just wakened up full of tears. Dreaming of when our Matty came to our house on her 21st birthday with a telegram telling her that her fiancé had been killed at the Salerno landings in Italy. He had been a policeman.

Victory in Europe was declared in May 1945. 'I have been dreaming of the VE Day procession starting at midnight walking up and down the avenues singing victory songs', she wrote. 'It wasn't victory for everybody though. There was a lot of sadness and tears'. To celebrate the German defeat, schools were closed, and the children were taken to see the film, *Henry V* with Laurence Olivier. 'Wonderful', she wrote in capital letters. But then again, my mother always had a crush on Laurence Olivier, ever since his role as Heathcliff in the 1939 version of *Wuthering Heights*.

Chapter 14

Even Haworth Parsonage does not look gloomy in this bright summer weather: it is somewhat still – but with the windows open – I can hear a bird or two singing on certain thorn-trees in the garden ... I certainly feel better myself for the change[74]

Over time, disorientation and confusion overtook my mother's forgetfulness and came to dominate her writing. List after list, naming past friends and family, continued to overflow from her diary on to anything at hand. Photographs, paper tissues, sweet wrappers and receipts – all stamped with memories. 'Remember, remember, remember. Don't forget, this is important' she scribed with pressing urgency.

Our Rosie's diaries often recorded the words, 'poorly day', 'weary' or 'pain'. When there were gaps in chronological dates, they corresponded to periods of illness. Increasingly, entries were made by family and friends, sometimes recording chats of times gone by and folk long dead; other times, there was just a line to let her know someone had been there. Outside the window and across the moor, the seasons changed. Never forgetting her lifelong hatred of the cold, my mother remembered winters of the past and how on one occasion she had to go to the Saint Patrick's Day Ball in her clogs because the 'snow was so bad'. Chartering her own weather forecast, my mother noted 'blizzards from the east' or 'rain from the west'. Snuggled up in a warm bed, our Rosie spent a sleepless night fretting about the weather. Noting the comings and goings of road gritters and ambulance sirens passing by, she surmised they were 'probably going Yorkshire way' which sparked another memory:

> 10.30pm an ambulance passed by. Hope no-one is hurt. Falls are easy done in this sort of weather. My mother had to stay in bed for several weeks one winter after a fall and had to have the bed downstairs. My Auntie Elsie looked after us.

Blue skies and white fluffy clouds over Haworth way heralded a new day and a sure sign that spring and warmer weather was on the way. Our bonny Rose loved spring and waited patiently for daffodils and yellow tulips to appear. The colour of sunshine and of hope, spring flowers brought thoughts of cheerful sunny days, of birthdays and the promise of better times to come. Relaxing into her frailty, my mother imagined that with warmer days round the corner she would be able to 'sit out' and enjoy some fresh air. In truth, she was too weary and 'made do' with the echoes of birdsong and a constant, well-stocked windowsill of fresh flowers and plants, inviting visits from an occasional butterfly floating in through the open window.

Snug as a bug, my mother surrendered to long days and nights in her bed, surrounded by flowers, photographs, notebooks and pens. In a state of delicate forgetfulness, she relived and repeated stories of the past. Having been a passionate reader all her life, weakened vision left her unable to read for more than a few minutes, and then... not at all. Moreover, even when read to, it was hard for her to concentrate in the present, and her mind wandered back in time, given any random trigger to do so. It was at this time, that Emily Brontë reached out with her poetry, bringing gems of connection to nature and landscape, so precious and vital to my mother's sense of belonging.

Will the day be bright or cloudy?
Sweetly has its dawn begun
But the heaven may shake with thunder
Ere the setting of the sun.

I read to her of 'high waving heather', the 'sacred watcher' that is the bluebell, a 'spell in purple heath', 'the violets in the glen below' and she would smile herself into sleep.[75]

Looking back through my mother's diaries, it is surprising to see that even with care and endless visitors she also spent many hours alone with her thoughts, memories and notebooks. Nights were long and lonely after my father died. 'Midnight 2am 2.15 3 3.45 4.25'. She recorded the time, again and again. Some of her writing was deeply disturbing, expressing fear and confusion: 'What is trying to get through to me?' 'What are you giving me?' 'Something is making me feel very afraid'. 'BAD DREAMS'. 'This is crazy 11pm'. 'What is this?' Spookily, there are three diary entries that read, 'your tiny hand is frozen'. What is this indeed? One can only imagine what this alluded to, but it sends shivers down my spine to see *Wuthering Heights* once again seeping into our Rosie's consciousness. But nights weren't always long and gloomy. There were occasions when she wrote happily of being woken by her mother singing or dear Frank sitting in the chair. At 2.20 am one morning she wrote, 'woke up flying over Istanbul at midnight. The river was all lit up. So beautiful to see'.

In the early hours one summer morning, our Rosie wrote, '4.45am I can see over the moors to Yorkshire, Haworth. The Brontës. Thank God for another wonderful day. It is a nice, bright morning. Mr. Blackbird nearly fell off his perch. I know the feeling'. I have no memory of my mother ever having any interest in wildlife or nature, but as she observed the world from her bed, no features of the comings and goings of the birds and the seasons were lost. It was as if, as life slowed down and shifted gear, she had time to be with herself in a new way. As a daughter, wife and mother, our Rosie's life had been lived at a cracking pace. There was no space or time for her to think of her own happiness or imagine life in a different way. Nor was there any expectation that she had a right to imagine such luxury. However, alongside bad dreams and tears, my mother found peace in watching the world go by. 'A blackbird looking for crumbs on the windowsill has made me feel very happy'.

In writing of the bonny squirrels, the doves sitting in the tree outside the window, of breakfasting with butterflies, of the calming stillness of the clear blue sky and white, fluffy clouds, my mother lived her dying. The happiness and distress that came with her dreams and stories were part and parcel of her dying too, perhaps gifting her with time to process trauma, to let go of unfinished business and to gracefully bow to a life well lived. In busy 21st-century lives, I cannot help but wonder when we lost respect and love for our elders and wise ones. Being alongside, holding space to invite stories of long ago, bears witness to history and blesses us with wisdom. If only we take the time to show up.

Promoting mental health and well-being is an ever-increasing and necessary theme in these times. Creating space to be with others and simply listen is encouraged and valued hugely. And yet, when people we love are near the end of life, or perhaps become forgetful and repeat the same stories over and over, it is often said that there is nothing anyone can do. What is the point in visiting elders when they cannot remember who you are? It may be scary, utterly heartbreaking, relentless and exhausting, and yet, sometimes, the only thing we can do is to be there, to show up and to carry on loving them. Maybe they won't remember, but, in that moment, perhaps we can bring some happiness. Simple intention to be present creates space for kindness and patience. Warm feelings linger after memory wanes. We do not need to know what to say. Chances are, 'you wouldn't get a word in edgeways any road'. Listening to the stories of our elders is enough. Sometimes, we do not need words to say I believe you, I love you, I value you and I honour the life you have lived. Sometimes, a smile or a squeeze of the hand is enough to create a peaceful sanctuary and safe passage.

I never knew that our Rosie's comments about ginger biscuits would be her last written words. Sadly, in what was to be the last month of her life, my mother's diary entries diminished and ceased as cancer, heavy pain relief and extreme frailty took an inevitable course. Poverty and rationing had been a hallmark of my mother's early life. In adulthood, she had both a deep appreciation and a 'waste not, want not' attitude to food, alongside a hearty appetite, especially for cake, desserts and peanut butter and jam sandwiches. In the last year of life, to our Rosie's delight, her diet consisted of her favourite butties, cake and trifle, but as the weeks went by, she could only manage tiny bites of each. Sticky rings from sugary cups marked her bedside table … cold coffee never drunk as her appetite and swallowing faded to sips of water, then nothing. Just sleep. Deeper sleep for longer periods became the hallmark of her last days. And yet, on the rare occasion she opened her eyes from sweet slumber and saw the faces of those she loved, she shone.

Chapter 15

Quietly as a lamb ... her life closed in a gentle dream[76]

Picture this, our bonny lass, lying in her bed, curled up like an ancient, hibernating dormouse, sleeping the days and nights away. Frail and skeletal, she faded. Her mind, unravelling, reordering and repatterning eighty-eight years of life. Sitting by her bedside, her battered and beloved armchair wrapped me in familiar comfort as I picked at a threadbare patch of faded fabric and rolled brown, crusty foam between my fingers, before flicking it in the bin. Such a blatant act of vandalism would have brought a sharp telling off from my mother: 'oi, madam!' But on she slept, never stirring.

In those final weeks and months, our roles were reversed. I became the mother and she the child. As she rested her silver-white head on my chest, I became the comforter, the nurturer and the secure, safe place. A warm, damp cloth scented with her favourite lavender soap, washed suffering and in her naked tiny frame, I saw my own ageing body. It was strange, as if I was granted a snapshot into my own future, and for the first time, I realised how much I am my mother's daughter. Always a prim and private person, her lack of inhibition became the most natural thing in the world. There was no embarrassment or shame, only gentle, loving kindness and the highest sense of dignity as I witnessed compassion and the best of humanity in the comings and goings of that small room.

I looked out of the window towards the murky, grey haze of the horizon where the moor and the morbid November sky were as one, as if drawing a veil between one world and the next. Breathing in the view of Boulsworth, I steadied my mind and stilled my restless body to focus on remembering why I was there and what I was called to do. Across the garden, a lone squirrel scurried through the grass and disappeared among the branches of the bare, old sycamore tree. Blackbirds and blue tits, their comings and goings so lovingly chronicled across the seasons, took their turn to settle on the metal feeder outside my mother's window, as if fluttering by to say a final farewell. I cupped her cold, pale, tiny hand in mine, caressing it fondly in the hope of committing to memory the waning feeling of my mother's touch. Tenderly stroking the folding creases of her working hands and the rough edges of her 'pillopatate' fingers, I sensed the harsh legacy of soil scrapped from the hundreds of potatoes she had peeled in her time.

Holding my mother's dainty hand in mine, an image of Charlotte Brontë popped into my head, and I remembered how, on her wedding day, she was 'like a snowdrop' in a 'white bonnet trimmed with green leaves'.[77] As she lay in her bed, her silver hair and marbled face framed by a white, soft pillow embroidered with tiny flowers, our little Rose was bonny to the last. As bonny as a snowdrop in spring. My bonny mum, what are you thinking? Where do you go in your dreams? Are you in a nowhere place, a void that floats between here and there, or are you young again, on the bus with Marion, tootling over the moor to Haworth? Are you playing hopscotch on a hot summer's night outside the corner shop or are you walking the lanes of home, courting that lovely lad of yours? Are you sharing a ha'penny ice cream with the girls in Dublin? Are you enjoying a picnic and paddle down Wycoller beck? Or perhaps you are four again, running home to your da, with a goldfish in an old jam jar.

Time was meaningless as she slipped in and out of sleep and memory. What was going on for our little Rosie as she lived her dying? In truth, we will never know until it is our turn. From a place of heartbreak, pain and fear, it is natural to judge that it is time – that enough is enough. In raw humanity, we may beg and bargain with God for suffering to end. But what do we really know? As I watched my mother sleep in a space suspended between life and death, I pondered if she was working through memories and reliving moments that somehow her mind needed to process in order to let go. And there was a lot to go through. Despite my exhaustion, I knew that death comes when the time is right for the dying and not for those left behind.

Through her stories and diaries, my mother had a gift of reframing her world by pressing the delete button on sadness. Our Rosie knew war and sorrow and chose to share gratitude and memories of friendship, family and community. Yet I suspected that for my mother, secrets, sadness and unfinished business lingered. My job was to be there and hold her in love until her work was done. Being with dying can be fearful and frustrating. As humans, it is instinctive to want to fix what seems broken, relieve suffering and make things better. But when there is nothing left to do, being with dying is an invitation to do nothing except hold peaceful space and allow death to come. That is compassion, and with it comes the profound gift of simplicity. At the end, there is no place for worn-out grudges and agendas; so often, they dissolve anyway in the dawning realisation that love was there all along. A few months before she passed, I was blessed enough to have shared one of those conversations with my mother. On a roll with one of her stories, she told me that I was brave and that she was proud of me. 'You could have caved in when you became a widow, but you didn't. You got on with it and looked after your kids,' she said. In that moment, it was as if I had been granted a rite of passage and earned my place in the sacred circle of womanhood. I had made her and my ancestors proud. My heart was full to bursting. I love and know I am loved. I forgive and know I am forgiven.

Hours flowed into days, days into nights and back again. My mother was dying. The primordial fear I had since childhood passed as I came to see that all was well. Her work was done, and it was time once again to wait for Dadda to take her home. She had loved and loved, and it was time to lay her tired old body down and learn to dance again. My mother had trust in her God and hoped for angels and loved ones to be at the threshold; I hoped for that happy ending for her too. Sitting in gentle acceptance, I had no agenda, questions or anger, only quiet gratitude for a mother who may not have always got it right but who always did her best. A mother whose commitment and love, mistakes and misjudgements made me who I am. 'Night night and God bless,' I whispered, echoing the words she had said to me a million times. 'Night night and God bless'… and I let her go.

Scrolling through Instagram, a few days after my mother's death, a post quoting the actress Whoopi Goldberg caught my eye. It seemed as if it was put there just for me:

> I realised a couple of days after she passed that no one would ever love me like that again. I wouldn't put that kind of sparkle in anyone's eye, you know? And you kind of know that those people are your first loves. Those are the first people you tell your secrets to. Those are the people that hold you when it's scary. That's a big deal.

And now for my shame and confession. Alas, dear reader, I wasn't there at the end. I wasn't there for her, and I missed the privilege of holding her hand, stroking her face and kissing her cheek as she took her last breath. I wasn't there, and for that, I will never forgive myself. I wonder if the churning in the pit of my stomach, the thumping of my heart, the oh-so familiar physical sensations of guilt that arise whenever I think of my mother will ever go away. As a nurse, I have been the one alongside so many people as they have passed, and yet I could not be there for the person who mattered most. Goddammit. In the book *Four Seasons of Grieving*, the author A. Lynne Wagner wrote, 'as a nurse, my head knew about death and dying, but as a daughter, my heart knew only that I had lost part of myself'. She went on to describe how 'I tried to grasp the finality of her passing and understand my new status as a daughter without a mother ... I fell into emptiness'. And with the finality of loss, she was challenged to 'find new balance and a new sense of myself as a motherless daughter'.[78]

A bereaved daughter, I was also the mother who 'got on with it' with purpose, to comfort my own children who were once again thrown into a world of sadness and loss. Still grieving my dad who had died the year before, I looked at my fatherless sons. I felt I had no right to grieve; nor was I sure I had the energy or resilience to go through it all again. Losing a parent at the grand old age of eighty-eight is normal, natural and an inevitable turn in the cycle of life and death. As a middle-aged woman, I had my mother's presence for over fifty years; yet the shock and pain of bereavement was real. I knew what to do. I had done it before. Instinct and remembering beckoned. I longed to walk on the moors, to stride out my grief and howl like an animal in the desolate landscape of home.

Clapper Bridge Wycoller

Chapter 16

though I knew I looked a poor creature, and in many
respects actually was so, yet nature had given me a voice
that could make itself heard, if lifted in excitement or
deepened by emotion[79]

A burning candle held space for loving intention, remembering
my mother, recently passed – my father too. Over eight years,
so much had changed. Husband, parents, an extended family of
uncles and aunts, now all passed. A black wool coat hanging in the
wardrobe reminded me that I had turned into my mother, who
always had a warm funeral coat for cold cemetery days. It is well
used. The Brontë stories, their lives and myths, were testimony
to survival, reminding me that I too had been there, survived and
could do it again. One day I would awaken, and hope, once again,
would cross my path. Like some sort of shapeshifter, I would once
again find a way to fit in to a world that at that moment was alien
and cold.

My children are adults now, and yet sometimes in the night, I
am gripped with fear and sadness when I recollect their trauma,
vulnerability and the difficult years they have lived through growing
up without their dad. I remember being told so many times not
to worry about them: children are resilient, they bounce back …
that they were fine. Then, as now, my intuition told me that is
not the case. All are clichés that speak of grown-up fear and lack

of understanding. Adults do not know what to say to children, so they say nothing and perpetuate the myth that they are okay – when in reality, children are silenced. Recent research reported that, for many, no one spoke to them about what had happened, and a recurring theme across the study was how little the children spoke of it at the time. Scared and bewildered, children felt silenced by the loss. Only in adulthood, often triggered by another bereavement, do they find a voice.[80] It was time then to check in with my kids. Their lovely Grandma Rosie died two days before the anniversary of their dad, and her funeral date clashed with birthdays and memories of burying their father eight years earlier. At the point of adjusting to life as young adults bereaved as children, when new paths were beginning to emerge, death once again crept in and threatened to trigger trauma, silent tears and anger.

Three hundred miles from Haworth and the moor, I held the grief and guilt in a lonely vigil and carried on because I didn't know what else to do. Writing to a friend in the Spring of her grief, Charlotte penned:

For my part I am free to walk on the moors – but when I go out there alone – everything reminds me of the times when others were with me and then the moors seem a wilderness, featureless, solitary, saddening – My sister Emily had a particular love for them, and there is not a knoll of heather, not a branch of fern, not a young bilberry leaf not a fluttering lark or linnet but reminds me of her.[81]

Unable to locate myself in a physical space called home, I reached for my blanket of Yorkshire wool and once again fell into a Brontë marathon, seeing with fresh eyes the secret mourners, their lives as adults bereaved as children and the genius it inspired. Knowing how much their voices mattered to my mother, it was comforting to imagine her chipping in with her own words of wisdom, sympathy and life's lessons, such as 'what children need more than anything is family, a sense of belonging'. My mother was lucky enough to have that in spades, but she failed to understand that it is not an experience gifted to all.

It is not unreasonable to suggest that poor old Branwell, battling with his personal demons, was unable to adjust to adult life without his mother, so traumatised was he by her death and that of his big sisters. But Charlotte, Emily and Anne, the surviving sisters, did find their voices through storytelling and poetry. In their brilliance, articulating the deepest and most painful aspects of human experience, they spoke of grief, anger, love, honesty, hope and faith. With a unique grasp on life and death, blended with wit, intelligence and plain speaking, the Brontës offer a timeless looking glass through which wisdom, comfort and common sense are reflected.

In different ways, Anne and Emily tell of the toll and exhausting relentlessness of caring. *The Tenant of Wildfell Hall* offers the reader a seat at the bedside of the dying. As a nurse for many years, I have been alongside countless people at the end of life, but when it came to my own husband, it was a different matter. All-consuming love and commitment connected us at a level I never knew was possible. Arthur Huntingdon's last moments in *The Tenant of Wildfell Hall* describe how Helen watched for changing physical features, listened to failing breath, the long silences, and the odd word:

> I took his hand again, and held it till he was no more – and then I fainted; it was not grief; it was exhaustion that, till then, I had been enabled successfully to combat … None can imagine the miseries, bodily and mental of that deathbed![82]

Ah yes, *that* exhaustion. It has never left me since the day my husband died and was my acute companion again in the early days after my mother's death. No matter how long I slept, I faced the day exhausted.

At the deathbed of Cathy in *Wuthering Heights*, the devoted Edgar Linton attended his wife, 'patiently enduring all the annoyances that irritable nerves and a shaken reason could inflict'. Ah yes, being there at the sharp end of anger and frustration, showing up, accepting the unacceptable. That is love. That is compassion. In her blunt, no-nonsense way, Emily wrote, 'his health and strength were being sacrificed to preserve a mere ruin of humanity – he knew no limits in gratitude and joy'.[83] Such is the brilliance and intensity of *Wuthering Heights*, a melting pot of the best and worst of raw humanity, honesty, enduring love, passion and compassion.

In the real world of 1848 Haworth, the Brontë family were to be struck by another triple whammy of death and grief. *Jane Eyre*, *Agnes Grey* and *Wuthering Heights* were published in 1847. A year later, brother Branwell, 'conscious till the last agony came', died. The trials and reality of living with him are there for all to see in Charlotte's letters. 'Papa, and sometimes all of us, have sad nights with him. His mind had undergone the peculiar change which frequently precedes death'.[84] It was believed that Emily caught a chill at his funeral. In fact, she also was in the end stages of tuberculosis and died a few weeks later, on 19 December 1848. Her faithful dog Keeper went to the funeral and howled at Emily's door for days. Five months later, the cruel disease killed Anne, her last words to her sister being 'take courage, Charlotte; take courage'.[85] Thus, grief-stricken and alone with her elderly, aloof father, the bereaved inner child that was Charlotte was once again isolated and abandoned. Her letters from that time reveal a devastated woman, deep in grief and mental anguish:

Life has become very void, and hope has proved a strange traitor: when I shall again be able to put confidence in her suggestions, I know not; she kept whispering that Emily would not – could not die – and where is she now? Out of my reach, – out of my world, torn from me.[86]

Our Rosalie was blessed to have two parents and the love of family. She lived through a war and saw illness, suffering and death. Was she a bereaved child? The answer is that I have no idea. In contrast to Charlotte's depths of depression, despair and anticipation of more loss, my mother's philosophy was always that of hope and of taking each new day as it comes. 'It's a good job we don't know what's round t' next corner or we would never cope' she would often say. These words of wisdom came to pass a few weeks after her death. My life tootled on without her in it. I thought I was in control, but then, without warning, my body let me down. Damn it all. Why didn't I see it coming? How could I be so stupid? How could I forget that control is just an illusion and the universe had it in for me all along?

Two months after my mother's funeral, I found myself at the receiving end of a car accident that left me with broken ribs. If only I had been able to see round that next corner. Ouch! Everything stopped except for pain and the stabbing questions in my head and chest – what now? How did my mother do this sitting-around, doing-nothing thing for twenty years? What is it all about? Is it a sign? Am I done? Wise friends said that I should enjoy an enforced rest and take time to recover from shock and the relentlessness of caring and of grief. Wearily, I acknowledged their kindness whilst at the same time wondering if I would ever be able to drag myself out of the mess or face the world in the same way again.

The death of my husband changed me forever. The death of my parents even more so. The feeling was that of being in a dense fog, separated from the world of the living, corralled into a space where only those who have known death of loved ones may dwell. In this sad place of knowing and appreciation, inhabitants see life through a lens that those who have never known death cannot envision. Hobbling around feeling sorry for myself, I palavered about the house, 'busy doing nothing' as my mother would say. Netflix and box sets became my new friends as sleep-filled days and nights became punctuated with every film adaptation of Brontë and Jane Austen novels known to woman; and my head, when not full of wool was full of nonsense.

Chapter 17

the sweetbriars gave out, morning and evening, their scent
of spice and apples; and these fragrant treasures were
all useless for most of the inmates of Lowood, except to
furnish now and then a handful of herbs and blossoms to
put on a coffin[87]

'I am both angry and surprised at myself for not being better in
spirits', wrote Charlotte Brontë to her friend Helen Nussey. 'As
to my work – it has stood obstinately still for a long while … no
spirit moves me. I am disgusted with myself'.[88] In the space of nine
months, Charlotte lost three siblings to pitiless deaths. One can
only imagine the pain and memories that were triggered and how
it might have felt to be the last surviving child. Her letters pour
out primordial grief and loneliness and make a heartbreaking read.
However, at the same time as sharing these words to her closest
friend, in the early days of bereavement, Charlotte was also 'getting
on with it', as my mother would say, probably because she had no
choice. Completing the novel *Shirley* in 1849, Charlotte went on
to produce what was arguably the greatest of her work, *Villette* in
1853. Her 'bonnie loves' gone she knew that life went on regardless.
Virginia Woolf famously wrote, 'I meant to write about death, only
life came breaking in as usual'.[89] Ironically for Charlotte, it would
appear the opposite was true. She and her sisters meant to write
about life … only death came breaking in as usual.

Acknowledging almost intolerable mental suffering, Charlotte, nevertheless, expressed her disappointment with the reviews of *Shirley*. For what it is worth, I applaud Charlotte for cutting herself some slack, giving herself some space to ponder what-ifs, happy endings and bringing *Shirley* to fruition at what was possibly the most painful time of her life. Always in the shadow of *Jane Eyre*, I think this book is hugely underestimated. Whilst it is true that nothing could ever surpass *Jane Eyre*, *Shirley* does not deserve to be pushed to the margins of Brontë history. As evidenced from letters written at the time, the way the author weaved her lived experience into fiction makes this a classic story of grief. Once again, Charlotte gives voice to the bereaved child. When there is no one left to fight your corner, to stand by you, the character of Shirley has a voice and demands to be heard. It is as if the author has been gifted a bereavement superpower as words pour out of her soul and onto the pages. This is ultimately a book about women finding voice and 'standing on their own two feet' – to quote another of my mother's pearls of wisdom. *Shirley* echoed down the years, falling from the library bookshelf, bouncing into Rosie's life and into the stories of all the womenfolk she knew. Against the backdrop of 'trouble at t'mill', there is frustration with men and their roles and behaviour in families, church and industry. Shirley is the character that articulates this furiously, the difference being that she has money (and therefore power) and thus presents an alternative world view in which men listen and she is respected.

In contrast to the joy of reading *Shirley*, in the wake of my mother's death, I found *Villette* almost unbearable – for this book is another kettle of fish entirely. At the time, my heart was broken. A heavied cold, stone-like pain was lodged in my chest. It hurt. The sad unfolding of events, scenarios contemplated only in my worst nightmares, had come to pass. As the dawn broke over Boulsworth Hill and the birds welcomed a new day, my lovely mum took her last breath, and I wasn't there. I wasn't there at the end. Viscous guilt, like black oil, sunk in the well of my lungs, and I could not breathe. I had not been there for her at the end, and that will never, ever be okay. Memory nudged me to recall that I must bow to mystery and accept that events unfolded as they were meant to. I was 300 miles away, comforting my once again bereaved children. It made sense and was the right thing to do, but it hurt all the same, for at that time I was a bereaved child too. I imagined my mother's soul, cradled in love and light, fearless and free. It is I who was stuck. Drained of all emotion and hiding from the world, I was a silent observer.

Now it must be said that my mother had no time for *Villette*. She simply did not get it. As a woman who had no patience with the miserable and self-obsessed, it did not fit with her view of the world or life experience, and as a result, never featured in her Brontë repertoire. Equally I cannot help feeling that perhaps she would have had little empathy for my grief and fractured life and would say, as she habitually did, 'now don't you go upsetting yourself' or 'chin up love'. As if I had a choice. My mother's value of choosing happiness, regardless of circumstance or the random misfortunes of life, was not always helpful; nor did it come across as kind or empathic. Whilst I admired her stoicism, rooted in generations of women with backbone, basing judgements on her own experiences meant that she was not always a good listener. Nobody had ever given her permission to be sad or grieve; she simply had to get on with whatever came her way, and she expected the same from others.

Reading *Villette*, I fell into the deepest matters of the heart, mind, spirit and soul. It is Brontë realism at another level, as page after page, the story delves into the darkest places of humanity. Without the slightest spark of self-esteem, the protagonist of the story, Lucy Snowe, is a lonely, broken girl, for whom life is a punishment. Unlike all the other Brontë novels, *Villette* is void of love, compassion and hope. Lucy is a crushed soul, and it is a grim read:

> Two hot, close rooms thus became my world; and a crippled
> old woman … my all. Her service was my duty – her pain my
> suffering – her relief, my hope – her anger, my punishment … I
> forgot that there were fields, woods, rivers, seas, an everchanging
> sky outside the steam-dimmed lattice of this sick chamber[90]

Lucy's negative, disgruntled view of the world creates an unsafe space
in her mind. Even the landscape, bare, flat, treeless, stagnant and
humid is a metaphor of the deepest places of grief, where everything
and everyone is negative, destructive and sour. With one or two bright
exceptions, the characters are nasty, suspicious and cruel. In *Villette's*
Lucy Snowe, Charlotte creates a character whose spirit is broken.

Letters written to friends at the time Charlotte was creating
Villette, suggest her own state of mind is reflected in the story,
again illuminating the genius of the writer. Brontë wrings out her
tormented soul to craft a classic and timeless psychodrama in which
grief and recovery is played out. So used to sharing her creativity
with her sisters, one can only imagine the loneliness Charlotte
experienced in writing *Villette*. As Lucy Snowe's narrative begins, I
ponder if Charlotte included a secret, gentle bow to Emily:

> Three times in the course of my life, events have taught me
> that these strange accents in the storm – this restless, hopeless
> cry – denotes a coming state of the atmosphere unpropitious
> to life. Epidemic diseases, I believed were often heralded by
> a gasping, sobbing tormented, long-lamenting east wind.
> Hence, I inferred, arose the legend of the Banshee.[91]

Of Celtic origin, the Banshee, the wailing spirit at the window, is an
omen of death. By including the legend in *Villette*, perhaps Charlotte
was invoking both Emily and the spirit of the child ghost in *Wuthering
Heights*. From despair to healing, Lucy comes to bury her grief and

unrequited love, once more suggesting Charlotte's own experience as she moved from acute loss to adjusting to a new reality:

> I knew there was such a hollow, hidden partly by ivy and creepers growing thick round; and there I meditated hiding my treasure. But I was not only going to hide a treasure – I meant also to bury a grief. That grief over which I had lately been weeping as I wrapped it in its winding-sheet, must be interred'.[92]

I recognised grief and saw it coming. The winter of my mother's death stripped me of energy and laid bare my broken bones and shattered self. Remembering that I had been there before, I knew what to do. In stillness and patience, I waited until my heart, soul and body could begin its healing. Like fledgling buds, tenderly easing out their baby leaves into the light of the turning seasons, the winter of my grief turned to the hope and warmth of spring. Exhausted from wailing grief and the mind labyrinth of *Villette*, I too cried out, 'the wind shifts to the west. Peace, peace Banshee'[93] and prescribed myself some poetry to soothe my troubled soul.

Chapter 18

May flowers are opening
And leaves unfolding free
There are bees in every blossom
And birds on every tree
The sun is gladly shining
The stream sings merrily
And I only am pining
And all is dark to me[94]

For six weeks, a peculiar, rattling *click-wheeze-click* sound accompanied my breathing whilst, in silent labour, my body got on with the job of knitting bones together. In February 2020, as physical recovery began to emerge, COVID-19 galloped across the globe and the world turned upside down. In a few weeks, everything changed as the coronavirus pandemic rampaged across closed borders, grounding aircraft, crippling economies and wreaking havoc with life in a macabre game of death roulette. No respecter of nations, age or culture, the pandemic threw all into the same boat. Some had life jackets, many did not; but all were swept along in a tumultuous quandary of grief, suffering, death, loneliness, unprecedented poverty and uncertainty. Every aspect of life changed, whilst the planet cleared her lungs and spluttered to breathe again. As the relentless background noise of cars, aircraft and trains faded, I began to hear, and pay attention to, birds singing.

As communities came together to support, care for and protect the vulnerable, I witnessed the best of humanity and ingenuity as new ways of reaching out to show compassion and understanding emerged. The human leveller of COVID-19 affected anyone and everyone, its toxic tendrils, baffling all with veracity, complexity and a new vocabulary of *social distancing, flattening the curve* and *PPE*. Strange and exceptional times indeed.

In *Jane Eyre*, Charlotte Brontë paints a vivid picture of 19th-century disease and poverty:

> While disease has thus become an inhabitant of Lowood, and death its frequent visitor; while there was gloom and fear within its walls; while its rooms and passages steamed with hospital smells, the drug and the pastille striving vainly to overcome the effluvia of mortality, that bright May shone unclouded over the bold hills and beautiful woodland out of doors.[95]

A hundred years later, as family elders were cared for, nursed and died in the front parlour of every poor home, our Rosie was also familiar with the rancid stench of the 'effluvia of mortality'. She too lived through times before antibiotics, when rampant diseases such as tuberculosis, scarlet fever and influenza took the lives of school friends and family. Her diary recorded memories of her grandmother's life too:

> My Grandma Kitty worked at Jericho Farm, the smallpox hospital. There was no NHS at that time. She was not allowed home for three months to see her children and she was already a widow. She had it when she was a girl in Ireland, so she was sent there to look after the poor souls. My dad said when he was young his sister Mary, fourteen years old, had to take part-time work to look after her brothers and sisters.

Fast-forwarding another hundred years or more from Kitty's life, and I pondered how much has changed. How far have we come in our ability to face our humanity in times of crisis? Dystopian images of windowpanes, framing pitiful imprints of lips and tears and hands; touching fingers through glass reminded me that, as much as I missed my mother, I was grateful that she did not have to live and die in a pandemic. It would have broken her heart to have been counted among the frailest and most vulnerable of society. She would not have understood the purpose of being locked away, shielded and separated from loved ones; and in her forgetfulness, the surreal and shocking turn of events would have confused and confounded her fragile self.

As a one-time nurse, I stood at the edge of my profession in grief and awe, as I witnessed healthcare professionals at the frontline of suffering, death and lonely isolation, holding the fort and the dying for all of us. Full of guilt for not being there, sometimes overcome with regret and remorse for the cumulative pains and injuries of the past, I had to accept that nursing took the best of me, and my body was at the time, quite frankly, knackered. And so, I took my place with the masses, stayed home and did what I was told.

In the hour of exercise permitted under lockdown rules, my daily walk took me along a river path where frolicking, fertile birds gifted a symphony of song. One unusually warm spring morning, the sun was already strong. It was one of those beautiful days, when suddenly, frost had been superseded by buds of hawthorn blossom arching overhead. Mindful and awake to the beauty of the unfolding season, I was at the same time irritated with myself and my mother. 'Ne'er cast a clout till May is out' she so often twittered and once again I was overdressed – hot and uncomfortable in a winter coat and multiple layers of thermal clothing. Approaching a graveyard, I reached out to open the heavy latch of a silvered oak gate. A sickly smell of stale beer drew my eye to discarded, crushed cans by a paint peeled park bench, where a grey pigeon perched precariously, waiting for his pickings of early morning worms. An empty crisp bag, blown by the wind, flapped on the edge of a broken headstone, breaking the slumbering silence. In a snapshot of a sun trap, an old ginger cat curled on a gravestone – taking a cheeky forty winks on the lap of Iris Mudd who was called to rest in September 1934. Scanning the path for people and other such hazards to be avoided, I noticed a couple walking towards me. As they veered away, I sensed their anxiety. It was a strange, new sensation, to be seen through another's eyes, as a plague carrier, a threat to other and to life itself. The COVID pandemic had made lepers of us all. I waved and said, 'good morning', but they did not respond.

April came and went and with it, a spring of glorious blue-sky days. Sometimes, my senses were hypersensitive and switched on to colour, light, smell and touch. The sweet perfume of emerging bluebells, the echo of a distant cuckoo and the tittle-tattle of nesting birds were moments in which my soul sang, that all was well and everything was as it should be. But most of the time, I did nothing. Absolutely nothing, except embrace my fragile, bonding ribs and try to breathe. When my mind was not blank, it was so busy it could not process anything. Drowning in a soup of sadness, bewilderment and self-pity, my eyes could not focus; I was, quite frankly, hopeless. Like Charlotte, at these times, I was disgusted with myself. When lockdown began, I clapped my hands together with determination. 'Right, now is the time to get that book written,' thought I. After all, it is said, Charlotte completed *Jane Eyre* in three weeks. In the hours she sat with her father in rented rooms in Manchester whilst he recovered from a cataract operation, she penned one of the greatest stories of all time. More guilt at my procrastination. But then again, our Charlotte was a genius and there was no Netflix or social media in those days – no excuses to be idle and pathetic.

Five months on from my mother's death, I was hopelessly sad, exhausted and wrung out like a wet chamois leather. I could hardly function and yet I did, going back to a strategy I used in the weeks and months after my husband died. Every day, I made a list of what I had achieved to check in with myself that I was still alive: got out of bed, made breakfast, fed the dog, walked the dog, loaded the washing machine, hung washing out. The mundane inventory went on, to prove to myself that I was still functioning and capable of achieving at least twenty things a day. Charlotte, in her northern common sense, big sister approach to life, would have had none of this nonsense, believing that 'labour must be the cure, not sympathy – labour is the only radical cure for rooted sorrow'. As her letters illustrate, 'work enabled her to retreat from the terrible reality of her own loss and the desolation of the life she was compelled to lead'.[96]

I began to write out my grief, remembering how on the night after my mother's funeral, I slept alone in an empty house, cleared of life and belongings except for my parents' bed. Odd how I wanted to be there for one last time, knowing that within hours I would walk away and say goodbye to my childhood home. I felt my parents' presence there, still, gentle and kind. Sleeping in that space was the most natural thing in the world. I was born in their bed, three doors down the street, no more than fifty yards away. The wheezing wind through a rattling window frame invited another memory of my mother. Cancer had taken part of her lung and, for twenty-five years, had left her vulnerable to even the slightest respiratory virus. I remembered the sleepless nights when I heard her breathless, restless struggle for comfort, sleep and air. Creeping into the bedroom, I would find her curled on her right side facing, as ever, the always open door. Leaning over the bed, I kissed her. 'Mum, let me make you comfortable.' And she succumbed like a child to my touch. I remembered too the dark winter mornings and five o'clock starts to hit the road before rush hour. 'Bye, Mum. I love you.' 'I love you n'all,' she said. 'Ring me when you get home.' These were words we had said to each other a thousand times. Locking the door and posting the key through the letterbox, I crept out into the cold and fog of a northern morning to start a long drive south.

I remembered too, after a night drive, arriving early enough to take my mother's breakfast to her on a tray. Her face was bruised and battered from a nasty fall, but her eyes shone with delightful surprise. She patted the bed to summon me to be seated, and we planned a leisurely morning and hot bath. My memory of that visit is a happy one, sitting on the bed with her, relaxed and chatting, talking about days gone by. Dad joined us and we watched *Oklahoma!* on the telly. Beyond forgetfulness, the three of us sang along, daft as brushes, 'The corn is as high as an elephant's eye, and it looks like it's climbing clear up to the sky! Oh, what a beautiful morning, oh, what a beautiful day!' At heart, they were a pair of old romantics and sang along together, 'Your hand looks so grand in mine. People will say we're in love.' It was not the wide and sweeping plains of Oklahoma but the wild, untamed expanses of the Lancashire and Yorkshire moors that framed their world. This too is my place, and the question keeps going round and round in my head: why do I keep walking away?

My parents always considered themselves rich because they had love, family, food on the table, a day's work and always remembered where they had come from. For sixty years, my father worked his fingers to the bone to provide for his wife and children. Like his younger brother Tony, he could shout and swear like a trooper but, at heart, was generous, kind and a true gentleman. A family trait it seems. He was of the generation that addressed elders as 'sir' or 'madam' and always stopped, took off his flat cap and bowed his head whenever a funeral procession went by. After he died, my mother said, 'Your dad would do anything for anyone and was always glad to do so.' And that was the measure of the man. In their old age, my parents often looked back from their comfortable home in gratitude. They had few possessions to speak of and left only a small footprint behind in terms of material belongings. Leaving their home for the last time, I took nothing with me except for a few photographs and my mother's diaries. With a tattered cardboard box precariously under one arm, I closed the front door of the cottage that had been my parents' home for donkey's years. Stepping into the car, I reached over and placed my treasures on the passenger seat. Companions in bereavement, the diaries of Rosalie O'Riley accompanied me on the long road back to reality.

Chapter 19

Redbreast early in the morning
Dark and cold and cloudy grey
Wildly tender is thy music
Chasing the angry thoughts away[97]

Dwelling with the diaries was painful, and in truth, impossible for the first year after my mother's death. From home, they journeyed south with me, on a 300-mile trek, back to where I live. There they lay, in a wicker basket in the corner of the bedroom, the dust settling like shrouded memories. For some reason, Rusha popped into my head, evoking a recollection of her opening a corner oak wall cabinet where she kept her best willow-patterned tea set and other precious bits and bobs. Breathing in the musty, lingering aroma of the past, she gently touched my head. 'I can smell him,' she said. More than fifty years later, I came to understand what she meant. As my husband lay dying and in the dark days of grief, I took his clothes from the drawer and held them to my tear-streaked face. In the vain hope of holding on to a piece of him, I breathed him in, bottling the memory of the man I loved. Lying in the corner, mute and odourless, my mother's belongings stared back at me. Nothing. Occasionally, I would reach out to them in the hope that they would bring her close to me. But the physical ache in my chest, the thorny lump in my throat and blinding, salty tears, cried out that it was too soon. And so, I waited. Then one day, towards the first anniversary of my mother's death, I was ready.

Of differing shapes and sizes, the notebooks themselves mark time, pink floral covers denoting birthday and Mother's Day gifts. On the cover of one is an image of Brontë Parsonage. In my handwriting, the opening page records our discussion:

Tuesday 31st July 2018. A new notebook. Nell has been to a concert at Brontë parsonage to celebrate the 200th birthday of Emily Brontë. She bought this book and a postcard. The postcard is the famous portrait of the sisters done by Branwell. Mum remembers getting the bus with Marion Turner to visit Brontë parsonage. There is a story that plumbers were working at Slyer's Farmhouse and found an original, hand-drawn portrait of Charlotte at the back of a drawer! The curate at the church proposed to her.

I noted that, during the night, my mother had added her own thoughts to this memory. Written in a shaky hand, she had corrected my entry, with an adamant TRUE, leaving no doubt in her mind that the discovery of Charlotte's portrait in the drawer was real and significant in its personal connection to her. For the umpteenth time, she went on to write:

Bus to Keighley. 14 years old. The Brontës and their stories have always been very special to us all. Wuthering Heights best. More true to life. She knew them all.

To stem the increasing tide of forgetfulness, it is evident in her writing that my mother was, as Virginia Woolf suggested, perpetually making notes in the margins of her mind. To keep herself grounded in a normality that was slowly slipping away, she made lists. The opening pages of the Brontë notebook, chart what I came to see as a pattern. Written in a familiar hand, crystal clear and coherent memories of parents, people and places of childhood coexist with lists and notes, grounding her in the everyday, echoing her unceasing, maternal interrogations: 'What's the weather going to do?', 'What have you had for your tea?', 'Are you warm enough?' In these entries, her writing is neat and legible, almost unchanged from the familiar hand I always knew.

9 am Breakfast
Window cleaner
Slight snow
10.30 Coffee. Fancy a Kit Kat
11.15 am sunshine
I have just eaten a Bounty bar
Dinner 12 noon. Cauliflower & peas. Sponge pud & Custard
SNOWING -where is my yellow cardigan
Dreaming of SNOW at the bottom of a steep lane. More like a nightmare.

When forgetfulness, disorientation and distress started to seep in, it appears that this was alongside episodes of pain and subsequent pain-relieving medication. In those moments, diary entries appear shaky, scrawled and sometimes illegible. My mother frets, 'I don't know what is real and what is a dream'. Often, she wrote, 'I have been woken from a dream' … and then goes on to ask questions such as 'Who is Guy Sykes?' or 'Is so and so dead?' Thank goodness for the internet, providing instantaneous answers to reassure. Guy Sykes was not a person, but a place (the street where her grandmother lived). The memory set her off spinning another yarn of how she remembered watching the blacksmith shoe horses on the corner by the White Lion pub and how herds of long-horned bulls were driven down Auntie Mary's street on their way from the cattle train. 'Off we go again with another long memory', she wrote.

Sometimes, our bonny Rosie would slip between memories and time. On vague days, she could not remember her address, thinking she lived in the family home of fifty years ago; but she never forgot the who's who of the family line. Copious lists of aunts, uncles and cousins. The dates of birth of her parents and their place in the ancestral tree, these were written time and again, not only in her diaries but also on anything she could find, until photographs, paper napkins, tissues, magazine and newspaper margins were full of notes and memories. 'Don't forget, this is important,' she reiterated.

In the night, particularly, my mother frequently recorded the time, suggesting that most nights she slept for no more than an hour or two:

11.15 fire engine. 1am, 2.30, 3.15, 4, 4.15, 5.30 PAIN, 6am, 7.30. Is someone at the door?

And there were moments in between when she captured random thoughts:

10 to 10 Cowboy time!
12.30 3.30AM 5.30AM
6AM 7.15AM Lots of birds.
Warburton's Bread
'GARDENS' Hanging Babylon
What is this?

The connection between sliced bread and the Hanging Gardens of Babylon is a mystery but then dreams take us to the strangest places. In fairness, most of my mother's nocturnal journaling made perfect sense. She wrote what she saw, and what she saw she captured, with the purpose of stemming the tide of forgetfulness. She did not want to forget the silver of a full moon, reflecting its bright light on wet rooftops or the daybreak dusting of snow over Boulsworth. My mother would often comment on the dawn chorus of birds outside the bedroom window, heralding a new day:

> The birds in the garden are very happy. A dove is taking his morning walk on the lawn. Lots of snowdrops. It must be spring. God bless us all! I saw a squirrel and magpie and tiny blue-tits – beautiful. There is a woodpecker in the tree.

One day on waking, to her joy, she wrote, 'All the snow has disappeared, and the sun is shining'. And my mother was back in the room, happy, warm and snug.

Despite her increasing memory loss, our Rosie could still identify birds and would enjoy discussing their garden shenanigans when visitors came to call. However, she had no grasp on days and dates, skimming over her forgetfulness with comments such as 'today is the day after yesterday and the day before tomorrow'. Throughout the two years of writing at the end of her life, the key players remained parents, family, friends and characters from childhood. Even memories of my father were of them as children growing up together, something of which she was so proud; 'We have known each other all our lives you know. Not many people can say that!'. And she was grateful, always grateful, ending most diary entries with 'God bless us all' or some such reference to the Almighty.

Chapter 20

I thought I was at home, she sighed. I thought I was lying in my chamber at Wuthering Heights[98]

Pondering her diaries now, it appears that there was a cut-off point. My mother wrote prolifically and repetitively about her life up to the 1960s, when she was in her early thirties and my eldest brother and sister were young. After that, memories of her other children are significantly less frequent and associated with what were probably traumatic events, such as the armed siege at the farmhouse on the hill. Over time, my mother fixated on this story and wrote repeatedly of how, in disguise, the red bobble hatted policeman made his way across the fields and took up residence in my bedroom, where he coordinated the operation with a pair of binoculars and our telephone. *Morse* or *Line of Duty* it was not, but this story ran and ran in my mother's mind, and she told the tale, 'from t' thread t' needle' to anyone and everyone who had a care to listen. There was an urgency to be heard, as if she was trying to process, understand and perhaps let go of something.

Reading again the many narratives of the red bobble hat siege, I cannot help but reflect on my mother's courage and vulnerability at the time. It was a scary day, and she faced it alone. This was not some rambling tale from a batty old woman. It was a metaphor for her life's purpose. It was the day she stood up, protected and fought for her home and family. A tale that became embellished family folklore was also a huge family joke. How we all laughed at the idea of our little mum being part of a police operation and yet, I cannot help but feel that in this tale, as in so many others, her voice was lost. In a paradox of opposing forces, our Rosie was both frightened and fearless in her mother love and overwhelming need to protect her young. Fast forward, and as her life hung by a thread, the sense of love and connection was as strong as ever. She did not want to let go. She wasn't ready to say goodbye to the greying middle-aged men and women before her, for they were her babies. She wanted to love and protect them forever, but the thread was weakening and the connection severing, as her earthly consciousness faded.

Our Rosie's big heart and love of children was well known. She was Auntie Rose to kids all over the town, who always knew where to go for a glass of orange squash and a homemade biscuit or two when their own mums were at work. As emergency foster parents in the 1960s, my mother remembered with love all the youngsters that shared our home, however briefly. But these were difficult times too. She spoke sadly of how a baby, born to Nigerian parents, came to stay with us and she was spat at in the street. I recall my moral outrage when I heard this story and questioned why she had kept it to herself for over fifty years. Our Rosie had no voice to articulate what had happened, no answer except to say, 'Folk can be cruel … so nasty.' In 1960s Lancashire, she did what she did best. She got on with it and carried on loving the little girl for as long as that love was needed. Whether it was this incident or another from my mother's catalogue of childcare, in the wee small hours she wrote, 'an old Lancashire Lullaby of a grandfather to a newly born baby to an unmarried mum':

Tha't welcome little bonny Brid
Tha' should na' com
Just when tha did
But still tha't welcome
Little Bonny Brid

In the frame of mind she found herself in, sadness was dissolving and bad things erased, as she relived memories, reshaped meaning and made peace with herself.

It seems sad to me now that my mother's mind did not have the capacity to recall joyous events, like the birth of her many grandchildren and great-grandchildren. Nevertheless, on seeing them, or when reminded by photographs or in conversation, she would simply shine. Perhaps the good things were a given, maybe there were too many blessings to count. It was as if, in a kind of grace, the people of our Rosie's childhood were seeping back through the veil of time and space to bring love and comfort and usher her through the closing months of life. They were coming to take her home. Above all, her paternal grandmother was a regular visitor in my mother's dreams:

> Just wakening on another day with my Grandma Kitty O'Riley, slurring down Bobbin hill. My Auntie Cilla and Auntie Maggie lived at the top.

> Just been dreaming about Auntie Mary living in Buckcroft, behind the Red Lion.

> I have wakened with a start from dreaming about my grandma, Katherine O'Riley, my dad's mother, born in Kilkenny (where the cats come from).

> 4.40 pm dreaming of my Grandma Kitty Riley. She said she was born in Kilkenny where the cats came from. This medication is affecting me, I am sure.

So often we hear how the dying see passed loved ones. It is easy to scoff, explaining it away as the side effects of pain-relieving drugs or simply dismissing it as wanderings of the doolally. Certainly not worth the attention of the living. Dwelling with the mysteries of the unknown draws me again to the fiction of the Brontës and their portrayals of soul-to-soul connections that surpass space, time and physicality. Speaking of Heathcliff, Cathy cries, 'he's more myself than I am. Whatever our souls are made of, his and mine are the same'.[99] Jane Eyre experienced the call of Mr Rochester as a sharp, strange and startling feeling, 'it acted on my senses as if their utmost activity hitherto had been but torpor, from which they were now summoned and forced to wake'. On hearing the voice of her loved one, Jane's powers come into force, 'I am coming! Wait for me! Oh, I will come!' she cries. Recounting this 'mysterious summons', Jane Eyre knows in her heart that it was real, it happened, 'In spirit, I believe, we must have met'.[100]

Bewildered and unable to locate myself in a physical space, I had no clue what was real. I have cared for many older people in my nursing career and have witnessed some strange goings-on. In *Villette*, Charlotte wrote of:

> mystery and peculiarity being entirely the conception of your own brain. The longer we live, the more our experience widens; the less prone are we to judge our neighbour's conduct, to question the world's wisdom.[101]

What I know is that the older I get the less I judge and the more I go with the flow of the unknown. Vivid dreams and visits from dead loved ones are not unusual. I have no rational explanation when the dying reach out and speak to their long-departed parents, but experience tells me to pay attention. I have witnessed how these visitors are welcomed, bring comfort and they do no harm. On other occasions, it is the living, the daughter, the nurse, the wife who bring solace. Where is the harm in taking the time to rock a dying old lady in your arms when she calls for her mother? Where is the harm if it eases her passing to believe her mamma is there? For many people, revisiting past events and relationships is part of the normal dying process. As a nurse, I know that when the dying reach out, smile and speak to the dead, it is time to show up with compassion and be alongside in gentle stillness. As the veil between life and death grows thin, who knows if loved ones come to take us home, but where is the harm if it eases the passing? A few weeks before her own death my mother wrote:

> Woken from a dream at 4.35am. My dad said, 'don't cry for me. Don't cry for me lass. I'm happy to meet my Maker'. 5Am Dawn is breaking. Thank God for it.

It was one of her last diary entries. I was not there when my mother died. I was not there and I think I will grieve for her forever.

Chapter 21

We were going simply to see the old trees, the old ruins; to pass a day in old times, surrounded by olden silence, and above all by quietude[102]

Our Rosie grew up with an innate mindset of service, of knowing her place and of graciously putting others first. As the daughter of this weaver girl, observing her always taking the leftover portions of food and the smallest slice of cake, it was as if she had no sense of self-worth at all. For her, it was what women as wives and mothers did. Pleasing the man and putting him first was what she saw as her role and keeping the peace, her most urgent purpose. As a youngster, I pondered with desperation if this too was to be my fate – and how on earth, I might ensure it wouldn't be. But tales of the past are just that. Tales. So often rooted in feelings of misplaced nostalgia, fiction and fact merge to become family truths. As the 20th century marched on, like so many young women of my generation, I lived a paradox, witnessing the servitude of mothers and grandmothers, loving them all just the same, whilst furiously rallying against patriarchy and desperately wanting to shake them out of their complacency. Ironically, the acceptance of their roles as wives and mothers was welded together with a steely resolve to survive and find strength and safety in womanhood, kinship and cynical humour. Perhaps their legacy and gift were a resilience and unbending determination that life would be different for me.

Always one to count her blessings, even in the muddle of forgetfulness, my mother's joy and gratitude at her longevity, of 'living to see her children's children', of being loved and being able to love – these were her benediction, especially on her birthday. From childhood, little Rosie loved birthdays because it was the one day when she allowed herself to be special and come first. Every year without fail, her children, friends and family responded to my mother's gift to self. Sharing the joy, she was showered with cards, presents, flowers, chocolates and cake. The first year without her would have been her 89th.

For the bereaved, birthdays, anniversaries, holidays and festivities such as Christmas can be the worst of times. My grief swung between a hefty void of empty exhaustion and raw pain, cutting through heart and lungs like a hot iron, triggering both tears and howls of abandonment. The night before her birthday, my mother came to me in my dreams. She hugged me tightly and we danced. Arms around each other, she would not, and I could not, let go. The next morning, determined to get through the day and to honour my mother as best I could, I bought flowers, lit a lavender-scented candle, ate sticky chocolate cake and remembered happy times. My gift was that of time, celebration, gratitude and remembering, but it was a fragile peace. One wrong move and I was in bits. One minute I was joyfully singing along to her favourite songs on YouTube – the next, I had collapsed in tears. Remembering that I had walked the labyrinth of grief before, to shake off my sadness, I grabbed the dog lead, got my boots on and set off for a hike in the rain.

Many years before, my mother's birthday coincided with a date spent with my future husband. We went to Haworth, where we shared cream scones and Yorkshire Tea in a café opposite the Black Bull pub. I wanted to stay in my favourite place with my chosen man forever. A solitary character, he never understood the need for belonging, hearth and home. We moved and set up home around the country several times in our twenty-three years together. He never fathomed my upset and would say that 'we are just living in a different house. That is all that has happened. Please stop crying'. As my mother's daughter, I stopped crying and got on with it, making a life wherever we ended up. The final stop for him was the undulating and gentle chalk hills and streams of the English countryside of rural Dorset. He is buried in woodland on top of a hill where the views are vast and breathtaking. Meadows of wildflowers blossom in the summer as far as the eye can see, and in this place of peace and silence, wildlife are free to roam among the dead. I am blessed to live in Dorset, but it is not home. It does not stir my soul.

Thomas Hardy lived here. We share a birthday. His grand home, a five-minute walk from my house, hosted Virginia Woolf for afternoon tea.[103] She came by train and would have passed my front door. I wonder what she thought of the red brick row of terraced, railway workers' cottages; and if she ever imagined that one day, someone would be looking back at her through a misted carriage window of time and saying, 'behind these walls, you live on. Your books are loved. They have changed my life. Thank you'. The places and landscape that inspired Hardy's writing are still recognisable. When I thirst for literature, the county museum is a stone's throw from my front door, and I can fill my boots with Hardy vibes. In the same way I trod the familiar paths of the Brontës, I walk every day in Thomas Hardy's footsteps. I have always been fond of the old man. As a teenager, lost in *Jude the Obscure*, *Far from the Madding Crowd*, *The Mayor of Casterbridge*, *Tess of the D'Urbervilles* and *The Return of the Native*, I could take to my bed, secretly sobbing in self-obsessed sadness of unrequited love. More than forty years later, Hardy and tears still go hand in hand it seems.

A year on and another early spring day was unseasonably cold, fine rain casting a faint cloak of mist. Black cloud bursts of heavy rain whipped a blustery wind, shaking newly unfurled leaves from their buds. With no route planned, my rambling took me to a small hamletted churchyard. Beneath a towering yew tree, I paused by Hardy's grave and pondered the role his books played in my life as a morose teenager. Inscribed on a tomb of Portland stone, it reads: Here lies the heart of Thomas Hardy. Bury my heart in Dorset, he allegedly said. So, they did. His ashes lie in Westminster Abbey's Poets' Corner, but his heart stayed in his beloved Dorset. I get that. Middle-aged, lonely, pathetic and homesick, I sat with Hardy's heart and cried for my mum.

A nudge of a wet doggy nose on the back of my hand prompted me to move on. Along the river and through puddled lanes, I came to a woodland of moss-carpeted ancient oak, beech, hawthorn and ash trees. Standing at a crossroads, with my back to a thatched cottage, my struggling breath and scrambled thoughts raced to catch up. To the left, a stone pillar memorial dedicated to Thomas Hardy. To the right a hazel, coppiced path, and facing, a bowl of lush heathland edged by rising pine forest. Above me was a window, and within the thick-walled frame, a bedroom, the birthplace of Thomas Hardy. Taking a breather, I stopped to drink in the view and to smell the freshness of new, emerging woodland life. Whistling to beckon the dog, I smiled, remembering my mother's hatred of the unladylike habit. 'Whistling girls make Our Lady blush,' she would ridiculously chastise, quoting an old nun from her own schooldays. Minnie the mighty hunter (in reality, an eight-inch-high wiry coated terrier) thundered through the deep, golden-leafed carpet of the forest floor and came screeching to a halt. Stroking her with enthusiastic praise, it was I that was reassured that all was well.

It was then I noticed a woman walking down the heathland path towards the cottage. Two glossy coated black Labradors trotted obediently by her side. 'Excuse me,' she asked, 'you don't know where I will find the Rainbarrow do you? I have been out on the heath twice, but I can't find it, and I'm scared of getting lost.' I confessed I had never heard of the Rainbarrow, but my heart skipped with excitement. Going on to explain that it is featured in Hardy's *The Return of the Native*, I realised that I knew it as Blackbarrow, the place where naughty Eustacia Vye lit a beacon to beckon her clandestine lover. Intrigued, I felt a literary adventure coming on – no longer alone but connected to something greater. My fellow dogwalker shared with me that every Christmas, as a treat to herself, she read *The Return of the Native* and *Wuthering Heights*. I disclosed to the stranger, now obviously a soul sister, that I had only finished *Wuthering Heights* the previous day. 'How did three daughters of a vicar create such awful characters like Heathcliff?' she asked. 'And how on earth can it be that it is so often portrayed as the ultimate romance?' I shared my mother's theory that there's nowt funnier than folk and that daughters should beware, as the world is full of Heathcliffs. We agreed that *Wuthering Heights* is the best novel ever, a work of genius in fact. I revealed that my lens on life now showed me that it is a story of grief and loss and one of the saddest books I have ever read. The lovely dog lady agreed. My new friend's plan was to go north later in the year for a holiday in Brontë country, but 'wouldn't it be nice if we could merge it with Hardy country,' she mused. We parted with my resolve to find the Rainbarrow and, if fate would have it, we may meet again under the bedroom window where Hardy was born.

Alone once again in the labyrinth of grief, thoughts of my mother filled me with the heavied feeling that I was just filling in time, until it is my time. A longing to go back home to Brontë country weighed me down. My head told me that it was bereavement, pure and simple. My heart reminded me that I would never share the fun of the Rainbarrow encounter with my mother. No longer would I see my mother's face light up or the sparkle in her smile when I shared bits and pieces of everyday trivia, uninteresting to everyone else but her. A tsunami of sadness threatened to overwhelm, and then her last words to me popped into my head. 'You don't need anybody to tell you what to wear.' Almost choking as laughter broke through a sob, my heart became brighter and lighter. From the dark place of 'am I done', my mother's voice echoed across the heath, 'Of course you're not done. You, lady, don't need anyone to tell you what to wear!'

Minnie the Mighty Hunter

Chapter 22

My heart yearned toward my native county ... whose verdure the smoke of mills has not yet sullied, whose waters still run pure, whose swells of moorland preserve in some ferny glens ... the very primal wildness of nature, her moss, her bracken, her bluebells, her scents of reed and heather, her free and fresh breezes[104]

The stir of a howling wind lashed my face with rain, and despite layers of dog-proof, water-repellent clothing, I was drenched to the bone. As Minnie started to resemble a drowned rat, my legs ached with the effort of plodding uphill in wellies that sucked and cleaved to vacuums of mud. Crossing a Roman road on the edge of the wood, I dipped down a winding, narrow path edged by wild yellow primroses, unfurling fern and bracken. Scrambling downward on what seemed like a dank chalk helter-skelter, trying my best not to trip over loose tree roots or twist an ankle in one of the countless rabbit holes, stress levels began to rise. At the bottom of the path, the Rainbarrow towered above me, dark and austere. In the first edition of *The Return of the Native*, the Rainbarrow was also described by Hardy as Blackbarrow, and on this bizarre spring day, it was easy to see why. The chalk earth turned to a light-grey mud as the footpath petered out into a vast, harsh, unfamiliar space. Immense pondlike crevices, carved out by heavy-duty forestry vehicles, blocked my path as if a metaphor for my befuddled brain and bewildered heart. In the woods, I knew the special spots, where light and colour were forever new and treasured; but this place was unfamiliar and disorientating. I had to admit that I was lost.

I was reminded of the moors of home, where there too, with one wrong turn, cherished, secure, familiar spaces could bamboozle and threaten a wandering soul. Of the path to *Wuthering Heights*, Emily Brontë wrote of, 'wading through heath and mud' and even, 'people familiar with these moors often miss their road on such evenings'.[105] With the Rainbarrow to my left, I surmised that if I walked in an anticlockwise direction, I would pick up a path. Minnie seemed to agree. In pursuit of a pheasant, she scooted around the edge of the muddy quagmire and, having no sense of direction myself, I followed her. Head down, I could barely see the landscape through the horizontal rain. But after half an hour of climbing over tree stumps and felled boughs, I was rewarded in my quest. Reaching the top of the hill, the dense clouds broke, and the dissolving veil revealed blue sky and warming spring sunshine. Oblivious to human intruders, wild forest ponies grazed nonchalantly. Through a narrow oak swing gate, the path took me through a tunnel of holly trees, and I stepped out onto the summit of the Rainbarrow.

The ridge of the Rainbarrow commanded the sweeping landscape of pine forest, blossoming bracken and berried holly trees rising out of the white chalk earth. The magnificent views of the valley below, and out beyond the horizon to the sea, blotted out the strain of the day, inviting a memory of coming home. With arms stretched out to the gentle wind and warming sun, for a moment, I thought I could fly. I had made it to the Rainbarrow. It was never that far away, just hidden down a path, a turn in the labyrinth I had never taken before. It was not Thomas Hardy who came to mind but my mother and Emily Brontë's poem, *High Waving Heather*: 'earth rising to heaven and heaven descending'.[106] After my husband died, it was as if the Brontës reached out of the darkness of grief to help me find a way through. In the same way my mother's cancer helped me when caring for my husband, his death and the consequent grief helped me with her – and she had led me to the Rainbarrow. Such is the great circle of life and death, the flow of past to present to future. All is one. All is well. I had done it before, this grief thing, and knew I could do it again.

The Rainbarrow and the heathland around Hardy's birthplace feature in several of his novels. *Tess of the D'Urbervilles* rested on the Rainbarrow and saw new patterns in the terrain below. *Jude the Obscure* passed that way too, but it is in *The Return of the Native* where the reader is gifted with a deep sense of the power and character of the ancient landscape. In the churned-up earth at my feet, I spotted a small, steely-grey stone in the shape of an arrow. Feeling the jagged sharp edges of flint, I wiped it on my coat and smuggled it into my pocket, imagining it as an ancient artefact, a symbol and invitation to be brave, to forge out the road ahead. The mound of the Rainbarrow is believed to be a Bronze Age burial ground and, sited at Thomas Hardy's back door, could only be a source of wild inspiration. For thousands of years, life and death had played out here. 'Pixy-led', 'the whole barrow was peopled … in a sky-backed pantomime of silhouettes'.[107] Spooky stuff, but grounding too. Like the backdrop to *Wuthering Heights*, in *The Return of the Native*, the supremacy of the ever-changing landscape is the central character. Desperately cruel, unforgiving, chaotic, passionate and wild, it is at the same time soothing, healing, nurturing, unceasingly beautiful and forever unchanged.

Like Emily Brontë's *Wuthering Heights*, one imagines that Hardy and his characters knew every inch of the Heath, the energy of the landscape touching their souls and shaping every inch of their being. Characters like Diggory Venn the Reddleman, Clym Yeobright, the homesick returning native and the ill-fated Eustacia Vye have the same magical Brontë-like quality of owning and being the landscape of imagination. Conjuring ancient imagery, Hardy writes, 'all that could be seen on Blackbarrow was a whirling of dark shapes amid a boiling confusion of sparks'. And I could not help but listen for the muffled clip-clop of a horse on dampened fern, the rattle of wheels on a stony path and the 'ru-um-tum-tum'[108] merry whistle of the ghost of the red man as he walked beside me in the labyrinth of the Rainbarrow. The surreptitious conduit of my imaginings linked a secret route in the map of my mind between the *Heights* and the Rainbarrow, and I realised that my new dog-walking friend was wrong. The landscape that inspired the Brontës, the Rainbarrow and all the special places in between that stir the soul *are* connected, for they speak of deep humanity and hold timeless spaces for love, life, death, grief, transition and healing. Standing on the Rainbarrow, my face was wet with tears – although I was not conscious that I was crying. I had cried so much and so long over the last eight years. I wanted it to stop. There was too much of life left to be lived. It was time for this native to return home.

I had lived away from Brontë country for thirty years, in several towns and cities and even more houses, but none of them had been home. In frequent visits to home base, the mothership, our Rosie always used to say that I had suffered from homesickness all my life. Married and with children of my own, I kicked against this assumption and her attempt to keep me a child. Surely homesickness is what happens to children on their first school trip. Grown women with lives, homes, husbands, families and careers of their own do not, and should not, experience such an ailment. But of course, she was right, as she so often was in her maternal intuition. She felt it in every goodbye hug, saw it in the well of my eyes and in the familiar, slightly over-enthusiastic wave as I drove away down the street and out of sight. My mother never moved out of her hometown or the circle of friends she had always known, but she knew about homesickness from uncles, cousins and friends returned from war, from Irish immigrant girls she knew from her mill days and from the evacuee children who shared her home. In the 1930s, childhood friends were taken away to spend months and years in hospital to be treated for contagious diseases such as scarlet fever and consumption. They knew of homesickness too. Some mill girls married soldiers, sailors or airmen and moved across the world. Some returned; most notably, her friend Peg who, widowed and retired, could stand it no longer and moved back to her hometown and sisters, to live round the corner from where she was born. My mother's diary records how, 'Peg insisted that her roots had pulled her back and there was nothing she could do about it'.

Perhaps homesickness could be defined as being the physical, emotional, spiritual experience of deep longing to return to our roots. Perhaps it is simply nostalgia, an illusion or yearning for something one can't quite put one's finger on. Pondering this (and in a synchronistic, timely fashion), I was drawn to a word that popped up on my Instagram page. Having lived in Wales for seventeen years, the word '*hiraeth*' captured my curiosity. According to Wikipedia, the words '*cianalas*', '*hiraezh*' and the Welsh '*hiraeth*', all translate as homesickness: '*nostalgia, an earnest longing or desire, or sense of regret*'. It is interesting how these words come from ancient lands and people, Gaelic, Breton, Cornish and Welsh. Perhaps then, it has more to do with a physical place, an instinctive connection to the land in which we are rooted. At the heart of *The Return of the Native* is the conundrum of connection and disconnection to the landscape of home. The handsome hero of the story, Clym Yeobright, suffered from hiraeth. His roots brought him home and stoked the imagining that life would be perfect from then on. He loved the Heath and appreciated the beauty of people and place; but as events unfolded, life's reality bit, as love and lust, tragedy and grief played out in Hardyesque tragedy.

The Brontë children all experienced extreme hiraeth, to the point where they could not leave home. In the short periods when they did, the consequences were devastating. For example, of her concern for sister Emily, Charlotte wrote, 'I felt in my heart she would die, if she did not go home'.[109] The root of their homesickness was complex yet understandable. Their elder sisters Maria and Elizabeth had left home to go to school, and they died. Knowing what we know now of childhood bereavement, one can only imagine that the poor, motherless mites were terrified, possibly frozen in this memory and clung to the safety and security of home. Nor is it beyond possibility that this fear, rooted in childhood, was carried forward into their adult lives and spilled out onto the pages of their stories. Was their longing for the security of landscape and home really a longing for their mother and for the family that was and could have been? Cathy and Heathcliff could not be parted from *Wuthering Heights*, even by death. Their longing for soul connection is an extreme attachment metaphor and voice of complicated grief:

> Heaven did not seem to be my home; and I broke my heart with weeping to come back to earth; and the angels were so angry that they flung me out, into the middle of the heath on top of Wuthering Heights; where I woke sobbing for joy.[110]

Away from home, the four Brontë children suffered illness and depression. They struggled to understand people outside of themselves and throughout their short lives had only a handful of friends. Perhaps for Emily, Anne, Charlotte and Branwell, hiraeth was to do with the grief of separation and a physical yearning for connection to the soil of home. Safe in this place of belonging, they could be themselves – bright, intelligent, alive young people full of possibilities and vision.

Spring turned into summer, and as the seasons changed, the Rainbarrow became my go-to place, where grief eased, peace settled and inspiration began to seep through the cracks of a broken heart. Dreaming that one day this native would return home, I was struck by the realisation that I had suffered from hiraeth all my life. From childhood, there had been a sense of longing for 'other', a desperate need to find a place of belonging and safety, a place of light, warm log fires and kind people. I knew the place; it was on a hill, with yonder views spanning out across the moors and beyond – just out of sight were, Wycoller, Top Withins, tea shops, book shops and peace. The literary tour of my life had moved me from Brontë country to Hardy country, but grief rumbled on. I belonged to neither the Rainbarrows of Dorset nor the green hollows of Boulsworth moor.

Straddled between the first anniversary of my mother's death and my husband's the following day, I was drawn to walk to the Rainbarrow. It was almost incomprehensible to realise he had been dead for eight years. So much living had gone on without him. So many other losses too. Father, uncles, aunts, all of them were gone, their headstones, like a row of dominoes, marking a generation past. I had come to accept death without anger or fear, understanding that my husband gave all he could, and it was his time. Even after eight years, there were days when sadness filled my head space. I had learned to let these days come and go with the flow of loss, knowing that it was my time to stay and to live and dare to find joy again. Standing on the Rainbarrow, in no woman's land, exhausted, bewildered and wondering what the hell happened, I stared, not at the view but at blank emptiness.

Chapter 23

Enough of thought, philosopher!
Too long hast thou been dreaming
Unenlightened, in this chamber drear,
While summer's sun is beaming![111]

With no knowledge or notion of what the year would bring, the new decade of 2020 heralded healing and hope for the world. Then came the global pandemic, and the world watched as COVID-19 wreaked havoc with humanity. Suddenly, it was as if my mother had died a lifetime ago, in a different age, in a different world, where we could come and go as we pleased. As COVID reigned and raged, new perspectives of life, death and grief emerged. With so much death, pain and acute bereavement, my own became irrelevant in the unfolding horror of wet windowpanes, framing pitiful imprints of lips, tears and hands. I did not have to touch my mother's fingers through glass or witness her death through a computer screen. I had known grief, but it wasn't that. Feeling I had no right to grieve for my mother, I buried it. Locked down and grounded in home and community, I watched and waited, grateful for the hour of exercise allowed at the time and missing with all my heart, home and Brontë country.

As lockdown eased, I was free once again to walk out my labyrinth of unravelling thoughts on the Rainbarrow. In a pandemic world, the pain of personal, acute grief eased, but the sense of hiraeth grew stronger. It was the kind of sickness for which there was one cure – to go back, to dwell in familiar places of comfortable peculiarity, to set the restart button. And so, after many months, Minnie and I found ourselves back in the mossy, green hollows of Wycoller. I could not help but recall childhood memories that echoed and channelled my mother's thoughts. Was I standing in the footsteps of Charlotte Brontë? Did she walk down the 'grass-grown track', 'between granite pillars', through 'close ranked trees?' Did she descend 'the forest aisle', through 'knotty shafts' and 'branched arches?' Did she stand at the threshold of the ruined manor house and conjure up the spirit of a blinded Mr Rochester? 'Can there be life here?' asks Jane Eyre. 'Yes, life of some kind there was'.[112]

The village of Wycoller, once earmarked for flooding to provide a reservoir to local towns, is now a conservation area and country park with willow-arched walkways, wicker sculptures of horse riders, information boards and picnic benches. The 15th-century barn, where, as kids, we took shelter in the rain to eat a picnic of egg butties from an old margarine tub, is now a visitor centre, housing an enormous rusty key that once unlocked the dark secrets of the ruined Hall. Seeping out from photographs and artefacts, the history of the place throbs with mystery. Yes, life of some kind has always prevailed in this place. Once derelict buildings, now exclusive homes stand boldly, archaic guardians to the skeletons in the cupboards within. A multicoloured, plastic For Sale notice flapped in the breeze, flagging attention to a stone-porched house that in the 1960s was tumbledown and abandoned. On this spot, Uncle Tony told us ghost stories, and one summer evening at dusk, we disturbed a barn owl hunting a scurrying mouse. Despite an exciting unease, I am still drawn to the beauty and charm of the place.

Humanity had returned to dwell in the once deserted village and yet so much was unchanged to the returning native eye. The precarious stone bridges, that for centuries offered safe passage to human and animal footsteps alike, still stood, safe and strong. The reflection of light on the bonny beck was the same – and yet, was forever new. As it wended its merry way from the moorland above, over green cobbled pebbles, sharp granite rock and rotund boulders, the crystal water followed the same route it had known for centuries. The deep and shaded valley of Wycoller is damp, even on the hottest days and the chill once again evoked the childhood memory of always being cold. I remembered how, in the summer holidays, we walked to Wycoller for a day out. Like the packhorses of old, my mother piled us up with sandwiches, fishing nets, swimming costumes, towels and cardigans. We fished for tiddlers and paddled in ill-fitting, stiff, red, plastic shoes, the cheapest that Woolies could supply. To the amusement of older kids, more often than not, I slipped on the mossed, cobbled riverbed and moaned all the way home – wet, freezing and in agony from huge blisters on my heels and little, mottled toes. Standing on the edge of the beck in boots and knitted socks, I shuddered at the memory of that little Wycoller-bound girl. It's no wonder she learned to wrap up warm.

The only sound was of birdsong on the early autumn morning of my return. As the sun hit the warming ground, a mist rose through a dense carpet of leaves, distilling a deep, sweet smell of earth and life and soil. A silver ring of sunshine warmed my back and like sleet blown in by an easterly wind, the autumn leaves fell and brushed my coat with a silent, crisp *swoosh*. In stillness, I stood at the gatepost of the ruined manor house and breathed in the silence. For at least five generations, my family had known and loved this place as *Jane Eyre*'s Ferndean Manor. Derelict piles of centuries-old rubble, stoned archways and abandoned buildings, so dangerously inviting to curious and naughty children, now carry safety warnings – a reminder of the prominence of this place. The wisdom and memory held in these stones have spoken, as if to say, 'honour me, respect me, for I am old and sacred'.

As if it were yesterday, I stepped into what was the hall and sat on the lichen-patterned stone seat of the semicircular fireplace. As Minnie busily sniffed the cold ground, a faint whiff of rancid urine and the earthy smoky smell of rotting plant matter leached into my nostrils and throat. That smell had not changed in fifty years. I thought of Uncle Tony's ghost stories and heard the echo of my mother's voice: 'Charlotte came to Wycoller you know – or was it Jane Eyre?' Did the Brontës play here as children, clambering over the same ruins my mother had done as a youngster? Did they sit in this place and dream up their characters? Did they wind each other up sharing ghost stories in this spooky place? In mind overload, it was hard to tell what was real and what was the phantom of imagination. As the early morning mist became a denser fog, a cold chill curled around me, and even the birds were silent. The slam of a car door in the distance reassured me that I was not alone in that ghost-infested place, as cold as the grave. For a moment, there was total stillness, calm and an incredible sense of peace. I always had the feeling in Wycoller that humans trespass at their peril, for they tread on history and dormant memory. And yet, this serene, tranquil and undisturbed place knows and protects its own.

On the hillside above the village where I used to play, now resides a 21st-century art installation known as The Atom. One of several panopticons resting in the Pennine landscape of Lancashire, the alien-like capsule has absorbed the alluring, creepy unease of the Brontë moorland. To experience the art is to step into a breathtaking, almost cosmic encounter. The modern, oval-shaped, metal-looking object is nestled, just out of sight, among slabbed vaccary walls that have dominated the land since possibly the Bronze Age. Eclipsed and yet overtly present and dominating, the avant-garde is juxtaposed in a vast, undulating, panorama across the Pennines to Pendle Hill and beyond. From the ovoid windows, I stared out, stunned by the wild beauty around me, my mother's words bouncing off the walls of the empty spaceship: 'You have always been homesick, our Nell'. No view in the world stirred my soul like this place. I had longed for it, dreamed of it. In this place, hiraeth was eased. The native was home.

The power of landscape is the beating heart of all the Brontë work, but it is in *Wuthering Heights* where Emily's soul is bare: 'my love for Heathcliff resembles the eternal rocks beneath – a source of little visible delight, but necessary … he's more myself than I am. Whatever our souls are made of, his and mine are the same, ... I *am* Heathcliff'.[113] Woven through the tumultuous relationships and complex personalities, in *Wuthering Heights*, the constant is the moor; like the river, forever new but always the same, a cauldron of love and hate, dark and light, heaven and hell, the extremes of human emotion happening all at once, in the place where ghosts and angels linger. Looking out from the panopticon, I was struck by the paradox of astounding beauty and creepy isolation. It was as if it was a secret hiding place, allowing me to become invisible, to watch the world go by, to spy and observe others without them knowing they are being watched. The moor, where the spirit of hiraeth has its roots – this place is who I am.

Like my mother in her labyrinth of forgetfulness, I could no longer see what was real. As centuries mashed and merged together in a dense fog of time, I pondered: who were the rightful owners of this place? Was it the Brontës, the druids or the wool weavers and traders who carried their wares across the Packhorse Bridge on the long path 'between Keighley and Colne'?[114] Was it the ghost of the headless horseman or the phantom of the drunken squire who fell from Foster's Leap, just yards from where I stood? Was it the Brontë children or a fictional manifestation of Jane Eyre and Mr Rochester who haunted this place? Or was it my parents and ancestors who had loved to come to this very spot? From the leafy green hollow of the Dene, I thought I could hear the echo of Uncle Tony's laughter and beyond, a resonate clopping sound of wooden clogs on the stone-flagged floor of the hall. Perhaps Wycoller was shrouded in an ancient spell, and I was watched from beyond the veil. Or could it be that I was the ghost and they were real? Feeling that nothing could ever be right or make sense ever again, the tears came. Alone on the hillside of my childhood playground, I howled and bellowed like a wounded animal until grief, at last, was laid to rest.

The Panopticon, Wycoller

Chapter 24

I no longer walk invisible[115]

The Brontë stories and connections to my childhood stretched and tangled across time; a forest of memory in which I could no longer see the wood for the trees. It was hard to tell what was myth, what was imagination, what was, or may have been, real, and what came from the dreams and fantasies of young Rosalie O'Riley. My mother's stories of the three sisters brought her life joy and new imaginings, and that is what mattered to her. The tales she created, the meaning and relevance they brought to our lives, how they shaped and supported in trials, loves and losses, were the musing of her younger days and comfort in old age and frailty. We were nobodies, from nowhere special, we 'walked invisible'.[116] But from this place, came brilliant women, and if they could do it, so could we.

For a mill girl of the 1940s and a bride of the 50s, family and home were everything to our Rosie – they were the benchmarks that defined her purpose. Living in the town in which she was born, surrounded by her own womenfolk, my mother was nurtured, supported and guided through the ups and downs of marriage and family life. A woman of her generation and ancestry, she thought her life was ordinary, that she had nothing to say. Like Jane Eyre, she believed she was 'poor, obscure, plain and little',[117] but she was wrong. Like Jane Eyre, she was intelligent, feisty and brimmed with passion for love and life. Her life and the lives of all the mill girls of those northern towns were extraordinary, and their story deserves to be told. May they no longer walk invisible. Our Rosie was one of a remarkable generation – there will never be another. Straddling the end of the Victorian era and living through the modern, they witnessed their world of certainty dissolve and navigated more change than perhaps any other generation in history; not only in the physical transformation of society but the moral and ethical as well. We may sneer and joke at their thrifty ways and irritating habits of make do and mend, of saving old wrapping paper, cut-offs of material, elastic bands and margarine tubs because they might come in handy one day. Then again, oh, how we miss it and long for those silken threads that knit family and community together, that somehow keep us human. As thoughts turn to climate emergency, it is sobering to know that they were right all along. If only we had listened.

Mothers are our first teachers. They show their daughters how to see the world. The lessons are always hard, sometimes misjudged and, at times, plain wrong; but it shapes who we are. With a fierce instinct to protect and equip her daughter for life, our Rosie made mistakes – of course she did. Unravelling those mistakes has been my life's work. And yet, through the labyrinth of forgetfulness, until her last breath, I know she did her best and never stopped trying. She was a mother who showed up and taught me to stand up, take responsibility for self and to hold on to dreams. A few months before she died, my mother took my hand and told me I was brave and that she was proud of me. I had earned my place in the sacred circle of womanhood and respect in my family line; but with it came responsibility, to carry my ancestors with me, to share their courage and to pass it on.

Following the deaths of Anne and Emily, Charlotte Brontë wrote a Biographical Notice to introduce the posthumous editions of her sisters' authorship.[118] In a letter to a friend, Charlotte explained, 'I found the task at first exquisitely painful and depressing – but regarding it in the light of a sacred duty – I went on – and now can bear it better'.[119] Through her diary keeping and storytelling, my mother walked a labyrinth of forgetfulness, passing on her life experience, love and wisdom. 'Write a book,' she said. And she shone. This book is my sacred duty to my Rosie, my mum, and to the women that have gone before. At the time of my mother's death, the Brontë Parsonage Museum had an appeal to raise funds to purchase a tiny book, the size of a matchbox, written by a teenage Charlotte. I donated money in Rosie's memory, to bring the book home to Haworth. She would have loved that. At the back of one of my mother's diaries, writing upside down, she noted that I had arrived earlier that day from the airport. 'New York' she wrote boldly. In fact, I had flown from Exeter. No matter, the thought gave rise to another brainwave:

'The Professor.' C. Brontë. Wonderful works of imagination.
No travelling by plane – whatever would she have made of it!

And with not so much of an inch of paper left to spare, she wrote, 'Full up'.

in the labyrinth of forgetfulness
the art of love and loss
wrap Brontë stories in
tangled wild beauty.
Womenfolk shaped and
shrouded in a dense fog
of time stir
silent empty space.

The Packhorse Bridge, Wycoller

Notes

1. Barker, J (2016). *Letters*, p 40.
2. *The Life of Charlotte Brontë*, p 216.
3. Higgins, C (2018). *Red Thread*.
4. *Agnes Grey*, p 144.
5. *Jane Eyre*, p 158.
6. Hoffman, A (2014). By the Book: *New York Times*.
7. *Wives and Daughters*, p 1.
8. *Cranford*.
9. *Shirley*, p 527. Here, Charlotte Brontë adds her own footnote explaining her choice of the word *reflets*, 'find me an English word as good, reader, and I will gladly dispense with the French word. Reflections won't do'.
10. *Wuthering Heights*, p 20.
11. *Emily Brontë poems*, p 13.
12. *Oxford Companion to the Brontës*, p 51.
13. *The Life of Charlotte Brontë*, p 236.
14. *Agnes Grey*, p 4.
15. Woolf, V (1931). *The Waves*, p 145.
16. *The Tenant of Wildfell Hall*, p 292.
17. Barker, J (2016). *Letters*, pp 134, 145.
18. *Shirley*, p 315.
19. Barker, J (2016). *Letters*, pp 66, 212.
20. *Life of Charlotte Brontë*, p 74.
21. *Jane Eyre*, p 281.
22. Barker, J (2016). *Letters*, p 29.
23. Barker, J (2016). *Letters*, p 132.
24. *Jane Eyre*, p 282.
25. *Shirley*, p 424.
26. *Shirley*, p 314.
27. *Wuthering Heights*, pp 90, 156, 158, 134, 293.
28. *Life of Charlotte Brontë*, p 23.

29. *Wuthering Heights*, pp 15, 77, 208.
30. *Wuthering Heights*, p 77.
31. Barker, J (2016). *Letters*, p 272.
32. *Life of Charlotte Brontë*, p 23.
33. *Life of Charlotte Brontë*, p 25.
34. *Oxford Companion to the Brontës*, p xxxii.
35. *Wuthering Heights*, p 325. The biographical notice of Ellis and Acton Bell.
36. *Wuthering Heights*, p 125.
37. Barker, J (2016). *Letters*, p 298.
38. Barker, J (2016). *Letters*, p 294.
39. *Wuthering Heights*, p 181.
40. *Wuthering Heights*, p 163.
41. *Wuthering Heights*, p 22.
42. *Wuthering Heights*, p 168.
43. *Villette*, p 258.
44. *Jane Eyre*, p 348.
45. *A Room of One's Own*, p 16.
46. Barker, J (2016). *Letters*, p 170.
47. *Life of Charlotte Brontë*, p 40.
48. Biley, A (2019). *Birds hold our secrets: a nurse's story of grief and remembering.*
49. *Oxford Companion to the Brontës*, p 63.
50. *Charlotte Brontë's World of Death*, p 4.
51. *Jane Eyre*, p 52.
52. *Jane Eyre*, p 56.
53. *Jane Eyre*, p 112.
54. *Jane Eyre*, p 112.
55. *Jane Eyre*, p 100.
56. *Jane Eyre*, p 102.
57. *Jane Eyre*, p 107.
58. *Jane Eyre*, p 326.
59. *The Life of Charlotte Brontë*, p 40.
60. *Voices of adults bereaved as children.*
61. *The Brontës: Tales of Glass Town, Angria, and Gondal*, p 68.
62. *The Brontës: Tales of Glass Town, Angria, and Gondal*, p 69.
63. *The Brontës: Tales of Glass Town, Angria, and Gondal*, p 69.
64. *Voices of adults bereaved as children.*
65. *Wuthering Heights*, p 91.
66. Barker, J (2016). *Letters*, p 138.

67. *Voices of adults bereaved as children.*
68. *Bereavement in Childhood.*
69. Barker, J (2016). *Letters,* p 240.
70. *Agnes Grey,* p 127.
71. *Agnes Grey,* p 6.
72. Emily Brontë, *Poems,* p 17.
73. *Shirley,* p 46.
74. *Barker, J (2016). Letters,* p 329.
75. Emily Brontë, *Poems,* p 14, p 13, p 27, p 24.
76. *Wuthering Heights,* p 147.
77. *Life of Charlotte Brontë,* p 422.
78. *Four Seasons of Grieving,* pp xiv, xv, xvi.
79. *Villette,* p 71.
80. *Voices of adults bereaved as children.*
81. Barker, J (2016). *Letters,* p 280.
82. *Tenant of Wildfell Hall,* p 452.
83. *Wuthering Heights,* p 118.
84. *Life of Charlotte Brontë,* p 275, p 273.
85. *Life of Charlotte Brontë,* p 295.
86. Barker, J (2016). *Letters,* p 222.
87. *Jane Eyre,* p 108.
88. Barker, J (2016). *Letters,* p 304, p 350, p 352.
89. *The Diary of Virginia Woolf,* 17 February 1922, p 167.
90. *Villette,* p 31.
91. *Villette,* p 32.
92. *Villette,* p 277.
93. *Villette,* p 462.
94. Emily Brontë, *Poems,* p 51.
95. *Jane Eyre,* p 108.
96. Barker, J (2016). *Letters,* p 240, p 241.
97. Emily Brontë, *Poems,* p 81.
98. *Wuthering Heights,* p 109.
99. *Wuthering Heights,* p 71.
100. *Jane Eyre,* p 444, p 445, p 472.
101. *Villette,* p 289.
102. *Shirley,* p 221.
103. Lee, H (1996). *Virginia Woolf.*
104. *The Professor,* p 191.

105. *Wuthering Heights*, p 6, p 9.
106. Emily Brontë, *Poems*, p 13.
107. *The Return of the Native*, p 36, p. 18.
108. *The Return of the Native*, p 33, p 149.
109. *Life of Charlotte Brontë*, p 104.
110. *Wuthering Heights*, p 71.
111. Emily Brontë, *Poems*, p 74.
112. *Jane Eyre*, p 455, p 456.
113. *Wuthering Heights*, p 73, p 71.
114. *Life of Charlotte Brontë*, p 25.
115. Barker, J (2016). *Letters*, p 246.
116. *Shirley*, p 257.
117. *Jane Eyre*, p 281.
118. *Wuthering Heights*, p 319.
119. Barker, J (2016). *Letters*, p 301.

Bibliography and References

Quotes and references in the text are taken from the following sources:

Brontë writing:
Brontë (n.d.). *Brontë poems*. New York: Everyman's Library (1996 Ed.).
Brontë, A (1847). *Agnes Grey*. Penguin Random House (2004 Ed.).
Brontë, A (1848). *The Tenant of Wildfell Hall*. London: Penguin (1985 Ed.).
Brontë, C (1847). *Jane Eyre*. London: Penguin (1985 Ed.).
Brontë, C (1849). *Shirley*. London: Penguin (1985 Ed.).
Brontë, C (1853). *Villette*. Ware: Wordsworth Classics (1999 Ed.).
Brontë, C (1857). *The Professor*. Ware: Wordsworth Classics (1994 Ed.).
Brontë, E (1847). *Wuthering Heights*. New York: Oxford University Press (1998 Ed).

Other key sources:
Alexander, C (2010). *The Brontës: Tales of Glass Town, Angria and Gondal*. New York: Oxford University Press.
Alexander, C & Smith, M (2018). *The Oxford Companion to the Brontës*. New York: Oxford University Press.
Barker, J (2016). *The Brontës: A life in letters*. London: Little, Brown.
Biley, A (2019). *Birds Hold our Secrets: a nurse's story of grief and remembering*. Watson Caring Science Institute: Lotus Library.
Gaskell, E (1857). *The Life of Charlotte Brontë*. London: Penguin (1997 Ed.).
Gaskell, E (1866). *Wives and Daughters*. London: Penguin (2012 Ed.).
Gaskell, E (1853). *Cranford*. London: Penguin (2005 Ed.).
Hardy, T (1878). *The Return of the Native*. New York: Oxford University Press (2005 Ed.).
Higgins, C (2018). *Red Thread: On mazes & labyrinths*. London: Penguin Random House, UK.
Hoffman, A (2014). By the Book: *New York Times* 20 February.

Keefe, R (1979). *Charlotte Brontë's World of Death*. Austin: University of Texas Press.

Lee, H (1996). *Virginia Woolf*. London: Vintage.

McLaughlin, C, Holliday, C & Lytje, M (2019). *Voices of adults bereaved as children*. University of Cambridge & Winston's Wish.

Penny, A and Stubbs, D (2014). *Bereavement in Childhood*. Childhood Bereavement Network.

Wagner, AL (2015). *Four Seasons of Grieving*. Indianapolis: Sigma Theta Tau International.

Woolf, V (1978). *The Diary of Virginia Woolf, volume 2 1920–24*. A. Olivier Bell, & A. McNeillie (eds.) London: Penguin (1981 Ed.).

Woolf, V (1931). *The Waves*. London: Penguin (1992 Ed.).

Woolf, V (1929). *A Room of One's Own*. London: Penguin Random House (n.d.).

Bibliography

Aynsley-Green, A (2019). *The British Betrayal of Childhood*. London: Routledge.

James, JW and Friedman, R (2002). *When Children Grieve*. New York: Harper Perennial.

Lock, J and Dixon, WT (1965). A *Man of Sorrow*. London: Hodgkins & Co. Ltd (1979 Ed.).

Miller, L (2002). *The Brontë Myth*. London: Vintage.

Taee, K and McNicoll, W (2019). *Surviving the Tsunami of Grief: For the Bereaved and Those Wanting to Support Them*. York: York Publishing Services.

Wright, S. (2019). *The Mother of the Brontës*. Yorkshire–Philadelphia: Pen and Sword Books.

Also by Anna Biley

LOTUS
LIBRARY